THE NEW ISRAEL

INTERNATIONAL THEOLOGICAL COMMENTARY

George A.F. Knight and Fredrick Carlson Holmgren,
General Editors

THE NEW ISRAEL

*A Commentary
on the Book of*
Isaiah 56 – 66

GEORGE A. F. KNIGHT

WM. B. EERDMANS PUBL. CO., GRAND RAPIDS
THE HANDSEL PRESS LTD, EDINBURGH

Copyright © 1985 by Wm. B. Eerdmans Publishing Company

First published 1985 by William B. Eerdmans Publishing Company
255 Jefferson Ave. S.E., Grand Rapids, Mich. 49503
and
The Handsel Press Limited
33 Montgomery Street, Edinburgh EH7 5JX

Eerdmans edition 0-8028-0021-1
Handsel edition 0 905312 46 5

Library of Congress Cataloging in Publication Data

Knight, George Angus Fulton, 1909-
The new Israel.

(International theological commentary)
Bibliography: p.
1. Bible. O.T. Isaiah LVI-LXVI—Commentaries.
I. Bible. O.T. Isaiah LVI-LXVI. English. Revised
Standard. 1985. II. Title. III. Series.
BS1520.5.K58 1985   224'.1077   85-4375

ISBN 0-8028-0021-1 (pbk.)

British Library Cataloguing in Publication Data
Knight, George A. F.
The new Israel: a commentary on the book of
Isaiah 55-66. — (International theological
commentary; v. 5)
1. Bible. O.T. Isaiah—Commentaries
I. Title II. Bible. O.T. Isaiah. *English.*
Selections. 1985 III. Series
224'.1'07   BS1515.3

ISBN 0-905312-46-5

CONTENTS

ABBREVIATIONS

DI	Deutero- or Second Isaiah, author of Isaiah 40–55
Heb.	Hebrew
JBL	*Journal of Biblical Literature*
KJV	King James Version
LXX	Septuagint
mg	marginal note to the text of the RSV
MT	Masoretic Text
NEB	The New English Bible
Ned.	*Nedarim*
NT	New Testament
OT	Old Testament
RSV	Revised Standard Version
SJT	*Scottish Journal of Theology*
TDOT	*Theological Dictionary of the Old Testament*
TI	Trito- or Third Isaiah, author(s) of Isaiah 56–66

EDITORS' PREFACE

The Old Testament alive in the Church: this is the goal of the *International Theological Commentary*. Arising out of changing, unsettled times, this Scripture speaks with an authentic voice to our own troubled world. It witnesses to God's ongoing purpose and to his caring presence in the universe without ignoring those experiences of life that cause one to question his existence and love. This commentary series is written by front rank scholars who treasure the life of faith.

Addressed to ministers and Christian educators, the *International Theological Commentary* moves beyond the usual critical-historical approach to the Bible and offers a *theological* interpretation of the Hebrew text. The authors of these volumes, therefore, engaging larger textual units of the biblical writings, assist the reader in the appreciation of the theology underlying the text as well as its place in the thought of the Hebrew Scriptures. But more, since the Bible is the book of the believing community, its text in consequence has acquired ever more meaning through an ongoing interpretation. This growth of interpretation may be found both within the Bible itself and in the continuing scholarship of the Church.

Contributors to the *International Theological Commentary* are Christians — persons who affirm the witness of the New Testament concerning Jesus Christ. For Christians, the Bible is *one* scripture containing the Old and New Testaments. For this reason, a commentary on the Old Testament may not ignore the second part of the canon, namely, the New Testament.

Since its beginning, the Church has recognized a special relationship between the two Testaments. But the precise character of this bond has been difficult to define. Thousands of books and articles have discussed the issue. The diversity of views represented in these publications make us aware that the Church is not of one mind in expressing the "how" of this relationship. The authors of this commentary share a developing consensus that any serious explanation of the Old Testament's relationship to the New will uphold the integrity of the Old Testament. Even though Christianity is rooted in the soil of the Hebrew Scriptures, the biblical interpreter must take care lest he "christianize" these Scriptures.

Authors writing in this commentary will, no doubt, hold varied views concerning *how* the Old Testament relates to the New. No attempt has been made to dictate one viewpoint in this matter. With the whole Church, we are convinced that the relationship between the two Testaments is real and substantial. But we recognize also the diversity of opinions among Christian scholars when they attempt to articulate fully the nature of this relationship.

In addition to the Christian Church, there exists another people for whom the Old Testament is important, namely, the Jewish community. Both Jews and Christians claim the Hebrew Bible as Scripture. Jews believe that the basic teachings of this Scripture point toward, and are developed by, the Talmud, which assumed its present form about A.D. 500. Christians, on the other hand, hold that the Old Testament finds its fulfillment in the New Testament. The Hebrew Bible, therefore, "belongs" to both the Church and the Synagogue.

Recent studies have demonstrated how profoundly early Christianity reflects a Jewish character. This fact is not surprising because the Christian movement arose out of the context of first-century Judaism. Further, Jesus himself was Jewish, as were the first Christians. It is to be expected, therefore, that Jewish and Christian interpretations of the Hebrew Bible will reveal similarities *and* disparities. Such is the case. The authors of the *International Theological Commentary* will refer to the various Jewish traditions that they consider important for an appreciation of the Old Testament text. Such references will enrich our understanding of certain biblical passages and, as an extra gift, offer us insight into the relationship of Judaism to early Christianity.

An important second aspect of the present series is its *international* character. In the past, Western church leaders were considered to be *the* leaders of the Church — at least by those living in the West! The theology and biblical exegesis done by these scholars dominated the thinking of the Church. Most commentaries were produced in the Western world and reflected the life-style, needs, and thoughts of its civilization. But the Christian Church is a worldwide community. People who belong to this universal Church reflect differing thoughts, needs, and lifestyles.

Today the fastest growing churches in the world are to be found, not in the West, but in Africa, Indonesia, South America, Korea, Taiwan, and elsewhere. By the end of this century, Christians in these areas will outnumber those who live in the West. In our age, especially, a commentary on the Bible must transcend the parochialism of Western civilization and be sensitive to issues that are the special problems of persons who live outside of the "Christian" West, issues such as race relations, personal survival and fulfillment, liberation, revolution, famine, tyranny, disease, war, the poor, religion and state. Inspired of God, the authors of the Old Testament knew what life is like on the edge of existence. They addressed themselves to everyday people who often faced more than everyday problems. Refusing to limit God to the "spiritual," they portrayed him as one who heard and knew the cries of people in pain (see Exod. 3:7-8). The contributors to the *International Theological Commentary* are persons who prize the writings of these biblical authors as a word of life to our world today. They read the Hebrew Scriptures in the twin contexts of ancient Israel and our modern day.

The scholars selected as contributors underscore the international aspect of the Commentary. Representing very different geographical, ideological, and ecclesiastical backgrounds, they come from over seventeen countries. Besides scholars from such traditional countries as England, Scotland, France, Italy, Switzerland, Canada, New Zealand, Australia, South Africa, and the United States, contributors from the following places are included: Israel, Indonesia, India, Thailand, Singapore, Taiwan, and countries of Eastern Europe. Such diversity makes for richness of thought. Christian scholars living in Buddhist, Muslim, or Socialist lands may be able to offer the World Church insights into the biblical message — insights to which the scholarship of the West could be blind.

The proclamation of the biblical message is the focal concern of the *International Theological Commentary*. Generally speaking, the authors of these commentaries value the historical-critical studies of past scholars, but they are convinced that these studies by themselves are not enough. The Bible is more than an object of critical study; it is the revelation of God. In the written Word, God has disclosed himself and his will to humankind. Our authors see themselves as servants of the Word which, when rightly received, brings *shalom* to both the individual and the community.

Throughout the past century there have been interpreters of the book of Isaiah who have stumbled over the proposition, based upon scholarly study of its form and contents, that the later chapters of this long book were not written by the Isaiah who is introduced in the first verse of the book. Other scholars became so intrigued by the problems arising from the composition of the sixty-six chapters that they concerned themselves primarily, and in some cases only, with the authorship of each of the many pericopes that make up "the book of Isaiah."

Yet the book is indeed a unity, not because one person wrote it, but because throughout its length it is an exposition of the Word of the one God. The OT as a whole is not to be approached as if it were merely "religious literature," mankind's thoughts on God. Rather, it is the Word of God to mankind and is therefore no less than revelation. The name "Isaiah" means "The LORD is Salvation" or "The LORD is Savior." Thus, with respect to these sixty-six chapters the whole book is well entitled. Isaiah of Jerusalem pronounced on this issue in his day and looked forward to a coming action of God to justify the name he bore. Consequently, two hundred years later the author of chs. 40–55, whom we call Deutero-Isaiah, interpreted God's method of salvation as he lived through the period that Isaiah had sought. Chapters 56–66, the work of a prophet we call Trito-Isaiah, thereupon announce, describe, and reveal the consequences of God's saving activity on behalf of his people Israel at a particular moment in the history of the world. He is thus God's instrument to open their eyes to see how, by grace, the LORD had now transformed his covenant people into what this last prophet in the book, contemporary with the situation he interprets, is in the position to call "The New Israel."

In what follows all references are to the text of the Revised Standard Version (RSV) unless otherwise noted.

—GEORGE A. F. KNIGHT
—FREDRICK CARLSON HOLMGREN

x

INTRODUCTION

The long book of Isaiah, with its sixty-six chapters, covers a period of some two hundred years in the story of the People of God.

We attribute chs. 1–39 basically to the First Isaiah, though that part of the book includes sections from other hands along with a historical inset at Isa. 36:1–39:8 taken directly from 2 Kgs. 18:13–20:19. Isaiah's active period ran from 740 B.C. into the following century.

Chapters 40–55, on the other hand, derive undoubtedly from the hand of only one author. We call him Deutero- or Second Isaiah, (hereafter DI) since we do not know his name. (See the volume entitled *Servant Theology* in this series which is a commentary on these chapters.) DI takes up the theological thought of his predecessor and develops it to meet the very different world that Israel by then had to face when in exile in Babylon. DI was undoubtedly a disciple of the First Isaiah even though they were generations apart. His unified document is an editing of the sermons he delivered in Babylon in the years 541-540 or so.

The very next year (539), after DI seems to have died, Cyrus king of Persia acted, albeit unwittingly, as Yahweh's anointed or messiah (Isa. 45:1) in becoming the 'saviour' of the exiles. Without a blow he conquered the city of Babylon and at once liberated all the displaced persons he found there from many lands. We hear of this act of Cyrus from the so-called Cyrus Cylinder on which he issued his decree (See J. B. Pritchard, ed., *ANET*, 315-16). The Israelites were, of course, but one group amongst the many. But as 2 Chr. 36:22-23 and Ezra 1:1-4 express the incident, those writers saw all history as being in the hand of Israel's God.

According to the early chapters of the book of Ezra considerable numbers of thoughtful, energetic, faithful, and dedicated

Israelites set about pulling up their roots in Babylon after fifty years' residence there. They prepared to return home to their native land, Judah, and to their beloved city, Jerusalem. Ezra's figures would seem to cover several caravans of returnees who made the long trek over the next decade or two. Those returnees whom we are interested in, however, are those who were the first to set foot on the ruins of Jerusalem ca. 538-536. Among these intrepid adventurers was our Third or Trito-Isaiah (hereafter called TI). We recognize him to be responsible, perhaps with a group of his own disciples, for this the third section of the book of Isaiah (chs. 56– 66).

A few years later again Cambysis king of Persia succeeded Cyrus and ruled his vast empire (which included little Palestine) from 530 to 522. In 525 he conquered Egypt, and since he would have to pass through Palestine to do so, he would have consolidated his hold upon it in that year.

We must use our enlightened imagination to picture the terrible disappointment of the first caravan of believing returned exiles when at last their feet stood firmly in the ruins of their ancient city. In theory they knew they would find it in ruins. But the reality was something else. Probably only a handful of them had known the beauty of the pre-Nebuchadnezzar city (before 586 B.C.). It would be largely the young and the strong who were resolute enough to attempt to recolonize their ancient homeland. What they met with, however, must have come as a shock to their faith. The city was by and large a ruinous heap. It had no walls, and the temple of Solomon was lying somewhere under the rubble. Only the massive stone base of the altar seems to have survived as a visible token of past history. What open spaces there were, whether amongst the rubble or upon the rock-strewn fields around the city where rebuilding might take place, were now occupied by foreigners and aliens. These had simply moved in to fill the vacuum left behind by the deportation. Naturally, this 'people of the land,' as they came to be called, were extremely jealous of the returning rightful owners of the area in and around Jerusalem. The returned exiles had the effrontery, in the view of these foreign settlers, to claim back their ancient fields and homes as their own by right. Moreover, those Edomites and Canaanites (the latter is a general name for a number of Palestinian groups) were all heathens. Since possession is the better part of the law, there did not seem to be any special person in authority to whom one could appeal for justice.

TI makes no reference to the person of Sheshbazzar, whom Cyrus sent as his commissioner to lead the Return. Perhaps TI had arrived before the official party could get there (as seems likely from Ezra 1:1). Or perhaps he was more concerned with his own group's theological calling as the true remnant of Israel, as he believed, than with political realities. Zerubbabel appears as the governor a decade later (Hag. 1:1). Perhaps Cambysis appointed him (had Sheshbazzar died in the meantime?) in 525 on his way to conquer Egypt. It would seem that TI did not live to see that day.

Also amongst the Israelite settlers were members of Israel's ancient priestly class. They had preserved the great ideal which that class had maintained throughout the whole half-century of the Exile. They believed God desired they should rebuild the temple and restore the sacrificial system which perforce they had had to abandon. But unfortunately this group of priests represented only one element amongst the total priesthood. Ezekiel, who had lived along with the exiles in Babylon, had singled out the Zadokites as the true succession that stretched back to Moses and Aaron. These were now jostling, we might say, to exclude other branches of the priesthood such as the Levites from gaining any significant position in the charge of the restored temple which they hoped to inaugurate.

Finally, there was TI himself—the leader, it would seem, of a party who thought differently from the priestly group. We shall see how these three parties clashed as they argued out their respective aims for a rebuilt Jerusalem.

TI drew his thoughts, as we have said, from Isaiah of old. The latter had vigorously declared that the Israel of his day was living in a state of rebellion (Isa. 1:2) against God's creative plan for his people; the 'faithful city' had, in fact, become a harlot (v. 21). If God was to go forward, therefore, with his plan for the redemption of all mankind, Israel must necessarily be redeemed first. For only then could God establish the house of the LORD as the highest of the mountains, so that 'all nations shall flow to it' (2:2). God's wrath against Israel for sabotaging his plan of universal redemption was such that the LORD must 'cut off from Israel head and tail' (9:14). To do this strange deed of love (28:21)

God employed the mighty Assyrian Empire as 'the rod of my anger' (10:5). Yet Isaiah was sure that 'a remnant will return' (v. 21). This was because, though 'destruction is decreed', it was 'overflowing with righteousness' (v. 22); that is, as we shall see in our discussion of TI's first chapter, it was overflowing with creative, saving love. But God would not bring this about from without, from up in the sky so to speak. God was to be known as 'Immanu-el' (8:8) or 'God is with us', as he had promised Moses he would be (Exod. 3:12). Consequently God must necessarily work out the renewal he had planned from *within* the life and experience of his people Israel.

In his mercy God delayed that 'end' (as Amos 8:2 describes it) for another century and a half. Only then did he employ 'Nebuchadnezzar', my servant, as Jeremiah called that heathen monarch (Jer. 25:9) as his agent in bringing to completion his act of judgment. This judgment fell in the year 597, when Nebuchadnezzar first laid siege to Jerusalem, and then again in 587, when he finally razed to the ground the veritable 'city of the Lord'.

But there was another prophet who lived through those terrible times, Ezekiel. He was a young priest, who most certainly possessed or had access to scrolls of the utterances of Isaiah of Jerusalem. He had been deported to Babylon after the first siege in 597. There he lived in devastation of spirit desperately trying to understand the ways of God with Israel. Finally,

> in the twelfth year of our exile, in the tenth month, on the fifth day of the month, a man who had escaped from Jerusalem came to me and said, 'The city has fallen'. (Ezek. 33:21)

From that moment onwards Ezekiel was 'no longer dumb' (v. 22) but was able to interpret how the saving love of Yahweh could be discerned even in catastrophe. This was because, in his mind and experience, theological idea had now become wedded to historical fact. Just before the messenger arrived Ezekiel had experienced that final devastation of spirit which came from watching his beloved wife die—at the hand of Yahweh (24:15-18)! Could there then be a meaning to her death? And so God gave him to discover that out of his mourning there could arise a new creative understanding of the ways of God. For some centuries now Israel had been regarded by prophetic voices as Yahweh's 'wife' (e.g., Hosea 1 – 3; Jer. 2:2; and later, Isa. 54:5). Ezekiel thus suddenly became aware that when Yahweh's wife, Zion, 'died' Yahweh himself—united with her in a metaphorical husband-and-wife relationship—had been 'with' her, as he had promised to Moses (Exod. 3:12), in all that she had been made to suffer. Worst of all, she had had to suffer the 'death' of all the promises of God within the covenant that he had made with David, with the land, with Zion—even his covenant made at Sinai, when through Moses he had said 'I will be your God and you will be my people' (Exod. 6:7).

Another generation now passed. An anonymous 'voice' (Isa. 40:6) answered the cry of the spirit of Isaiah of old, this time from out of the desolation of the Babylonian exile. It offered the assurance that while creation certainly withers like grass, 'the word of our God will stand for ever' (v. 8).

So from the book of Isaiah, chs. 40 – 55, we learn that Yahweh refused to let his people accept the idea that he had 'divorced' his bride, Israel (50:1). Consequently he is still Israel's Immanuel, 'God with us'. In fact, DI goes further and expresses the still more daring proposition which he puts in the mouth of heathen bystanders:

> God is *in* you only. Truly, O God of Israel, the Saviour, thou art a God who hidest thyself. (45:14-15 author's translation)

The inference is, of course, that God does what no other god does: he hides himself in the husband-and-wife relationship through his extraordinary self-identification with his sinful, erring, rebellious bride. This means that, as saviour, he saves actually from within the situation with which he has identified himself, and not from outside of it.

Again, DI waxed lyrical about the new Jerusalem to come, which God would bring in from within, and through, and by means of the suffering of the Exile. His poetry at times employed apocalyptic language; or rather, as we shall examine later, DI had come to see the restored Jerusalem in an eschatological light (54:11-13). As an element in that vision Jerusalem's inhabitants, in conformity with God's promise to Abraham (Gen. 12:1-3), would again multiply to fill to capacity both the Holy City and all the other cities of the Holy Land (Isa. 54:1-3).

DI had spoken thus before the event actually occurred which Ezekiel had earlier portrayed as the coming 'resurrection' of Israel (Ezek. 37). DI had spoken in faith that this thing would certainly eventuate. But now, in TI's view, this 'resurrection' was a thing of the past. Israel had been raised from the grave, in that God had now used his 'messiah' Cyrus to inaugurate the whole new future for this people whom God himself now called 'the New Israel'. Gerhard von Rad would go further than this. In his *Old Testament Theology* (2:246) he sees the birth of the New Israel as taking place, not so much at the moment of Cyrus' edict as actually in the promise of it that preceded the event, as recorded at Isa. 43:18ff. This is because, as von Rad says, it is not events in history that are decisive in themselves, but the purpose and promise of God with respect to those events.

It was now a historical reality that God had breathed new life into those dry bones.

> And you shall know that I am the LORD, when I open your graves. . . . And I will put my Spirit within you, and you shall live, and I will place you in your own land. (Ezek. 37:13-14)

The ideas of Isaiah were now no mere speculative theology; the declaration that 'the LORD saves' (the meaning of the name Isaiah) had now become 'flesh' in this extraordinary manner. TI has thus recognized that the pattern of God's saving, recreative activity is now a matter of record.

A retiring president of the American Society of Biblical Literature once declared in his valedictory address: 'We Old Testament scholars must first of all be historians'.

To declare that the first returnees reached Jerusalem shortly after the promulgation of Cyrus' decree is to make a historical statement. In the case of the works of TI we must begin with that fact. The belief that Cyrus was God's instrument and that he occasioned what Ezekiel described as the 'resurrection' (Ezekiel 37) of the dry bones of Israel from the 'death' of the Exile, and that it was God himself who gave the name of the New Israel to these bewildered returnees are all statements of faith; however, they all depend upon the exactitude of historical research.

But TI goes further than this in his theological reasoning. He sees the Return to be of eschatological significance — that is, as an event rooted, not first of all in history, but primarily in eternity. Because of this order of thought, TI sees this moment in history as revelation of what is in the heart of the living God. He sees the 'resurrection' of Israel as a historical moment from which God reveals to Israel an aspect of his purpose and plan as Saviour. Stanley Brice Frost would express this concept in these words: 'The historical does not merely give warning of the eschatological, but is in some sense the expression within history and time of that event which does not itself belong to time and sequence' (*Old Testament Apocalyptic*, 55). This means that, in the case, for example, of the rebirth of Zion, what we learn of in TI is actually the firstfruits of a revelation that could take place again and again in Israel's story, and that is in fact creating in eternity that which is being revealed.

TI's theology is thus in conformity with that of Jesus. In Jesus' parable of the great judgment (Matt. 25:31-46) or, perhaps better, by means of his simple pictorial theology such as we hear from his lips at 18:10, we see the total relationship between events in history and eternal reality. Thus the apocalyptic we meet with in TI is an illustration in parable form of the essence of eschatology. He was aware, to use Jesus' language, that 'The kingdom of God is here with you now (*entos hymon*)' (Luke 17:21 author's translation). For the kingdom is the sacramental presence that is declared in the name Isaiah.

CHAPTER 56

THE CONTENT OF
THE COVENANT
Isaiah 56:1-12

1-2a This third part of the book of Isaiah begins with TI actually putting into the mouth of God a declaration of what God expects of his 'resurrected' and forgiven people, as they take up their new life in the ruins of their old city. God's expectation of them is to be lived out within the context of the social situation that prevailed in the decade 538-530 or so, a period which was very different in quality both from life in old Jerusalem before 586 and from their experience of life in the Babylonian exile.

God's Word to the returnees is expressed in a compact utterance: 'Keep justice, and do righteousness'. This had, of course, long since been expressed as God's Word in the Torah, the Five Books of Moses. But now the basic content of God's Word is summarized in these terms in face of a wholly new historical situation. The people who were now present with our prophet were evidently unable to grasp the historical fact that God's 'salvation' had now actually come. TI had learned this way of speaking from DI, where it is expressed proleptically at Isa. 43:1. As they gazed around them at the ruins of the former beautiful city of Jerusalem the people could be excused for not understanding the reality of grace. Their task, it seemed, was to show their contemporaries that God's salvation must be grasped in faith. They were to realize that God had now acted first, whereupon it was their responsibility to work out the significance of what God had done by obeying his word in action.

'Keep' (or better, 'guard') 'justice' is God's first requirement. In any Hebrew sentence the word or idea most to be emphasised is placed first. The pietists amongst TI's hearers may well have been disappointed at hearing how the first requirement laid upon

1

the returned community was to learn that membership in the Covenant demanded social responsibility. It had been so before the destruction of Jerusalem, as Amos, for example, had insisted. In continuity therefore with the old, and despite the completely new sociological conditions in which they found themselves, TI shows that this command still comes first as it must always, even today; in that, we too are members of this 'postresurrection' community. Later in his address we discover to whom justice is to be given. It is not to be confined to one's own inner circle of family and friends. It is to be 'guarded' and thus valued as God's will, and is to be extended to all people everywhere. The command here issues from the mouth of God, for God himself is the God of justice, compassionately concerned for the poor and needy, for the desolate and those who mourn.

How greatly the instruction 'and do righteousness' is misunderstood, particularly in today's world. In the popular mind, 'righteousness' has come to mean 'self-righteousness', or 'living a good and moral life', and even being aware and proud of doing so. On the other hand, through the Middle Ages 'justice' was the normal Latin translation for the Hebrew word that occurs here (*tsedaqah*), rendering the idea of righteousness as 'a man's proper conduct over against an absolute ethical norm' (G. von Rad, *Old Testament Theology*, 1:370-71).

The whole long book of Isaiah, covering as it does a period of more than two hundred years of the history of God's saving love, makes use of two forms of the word for 'righteous'. These are the masculine form *tsedeq* and the feminine form *tsedaqah*. It is important to note the difference between them. Isaiah of Jerusalem first used *tsedeq* to describe God's saving, creative activity, his 'putting right' his people Israel, his putting them in a right relationship with himself. This he had done in the early days when he had rescued them from the power of Pharaoh and thereafter offered them, through the laws of the covenant he gave them at Sinai, the means of living continually in a right relationship with himself. Hosea 2:18-20 tells how God planned to take his people back though they had rebelled against him, thus seeing God's covenant faithfulness as more than just a physical rescue from slavery. It was to be seen in terms of God's steadfast love and complete forgiveness: 'I will make for you a covenant. . . . And I will betroth you to me for ever in righteousness (*tsedeq*, God's

2

act of redemption) and in justice (*mishpat*)'. 'Justice' comes first in TI's declaration; before him Amos had considered it to be basically important. Hosea continues: 'in steadfast love (*hesed*, God's covenantal love that never lets go) and (finally) in mercy (*rahamim*, a word that speaks of the deep physical love a woman has for the child of her womb, *rehem*)'. These Hebrew words all describe actions of God.

Returning to Isa. 56:1, we note God's command to the newly restored people of the Covenant, in the light of what he has now done for them. This command expresses what they in their turn are to do to uphold their side of the Covenant in the new situation. To maintain the Covenant, Israel is to do what God does, that is, they are to 'do righteousness'. This time, however, the word is not *tsedeq*, the word that describes God's action; it is *tsedaqah*. Two centuries earlier Isaiah had isolated this feminine noun and used it to describe that creative, loving activity between persons that has been inspired and empowered by God's initial act of *tsedeq*; and this meaning of the word had continued throughout DI's collection of oracles into those of TI.

Beginning with this period of the Return, the feminine noun *tsedaqah* began to move in meaning in two directions. Amongst those who had never experienced God's *tsedeq* because they had remained in exile and had perhaps become scattered throughout the Persian Empire (see the book of Esther), *tsedaqah* came to describe a mere act of benevolence, one good deed in a naughty world. Later still the prophet Mohammed grasped the cognate term in the Arabic language and employed it in the Koran to describe the act of giving alms to the poor. Almsgiving then actually became mandatory in his system and since then has always been one of the pillars of the Islamic faith. But for those who had returned to Zion, and for those in turn who lived there after them, the word *tsedaqah* described something you do unto others as God has already done unto you. It becomes, first, an act of compassionate love, such as is giving a cup of cold water to a thirsty person. But second, since it is *God's tsedaqah*, though *done* by humans, the word describes any creative activity by which a covenant member can woo a sinner out of his or her folly into commitment to Yahweh.

We are to remember that the LXX, the Greek translation of the OT made some centuries before Christ and which was at

hand for the early Christian Church to use, was seldom consistent
in rendering these two Hebrew words. As Theodore Henry Rob-
inson declared with reference to the NEB: 'The most fascinating
thing about translating is that it is so impossible'. The usual
translation in the LXX for both *tsedeq* and *tsedaqah* is the one
word *dikaiosyne*. Thus we are obliged to be very careful when
seeking to understand Paul's use of the term in his Letter to the
Romans and elsewhere. In fact,

> interpreters are still not agreed whether Paul's use of "righ-
> teousness of God" refers to an attribute of God by which
> he acts according to justice (genitive of possession) or to
> something which he gives to man (genitive of origin). . . .
> In any case, it is clear that in Paul "righteousness" defi-
> nitely refers to salvation and redemption,

writes Hendrikus Berkhof (*Christian Faith*, 127).

One strand in postexilic Judaism, however, held fast to the
Isaian meaning of *tsedaqah*. The Mishnah (*Aboth* i.12) informs us
that Simeon the Just, long before its day, had summarized the
faith in these words: 'By three things is the world sustained: by
the Torah, by the (temple) service, and by deeds of lovingkind-
ness'. This Simeon was either Simeon, son of Onias and high
priest about 280 B.C., or he was Simeon II, high priest about
200 B.C.

We note, finally, in v. 1, that God himself declares: 'Soon my
salvation (*yeshu'ah*, a feminine noun) will come, and my deliverance (*tsedaqah*, also feminine) be revealed'. God's saving act is
usually described by the masculine form of this word, *yesha'*, in
parallel with *tsedeq*. But now, in parallel with *tsedaqah*, we see that
God's saving love is not a mere theological idea, but is something
that is true only when it comes to fruition, or only when we see
God's deliverance being acted out by those who have accepted
it in their own lives.

The Sabbath an Instrument of Mission (2b-8)

In the Torah we find that the sabbath was God's gift to his
covenant people. As v. 4 puts it, they are 'my sabbaths', not
Israel's. Persians, Babylonians, Canaanites, Egyptians, Greeks—
none of these ever thought of 'stopping' work (as the word means
literally) one day in seven so as to give ordinary people, the

4

masses of humanity, a complete day of rest. Keeping *God's* sabbath meant, moreover, that those same common folk might be taught to possess a God-centred theology, one in which every seemingly unimportant human being could become God's instrument for human happiness and success (cf. Matt. 12:12). TI makes no reference here to the keeping of the Ten Commandments. What he does emphasise is obedience to God's will with its issue in practical love. Thus even the sabbath becomes for him an instrument of God's redemptive love (*tsedeq*), as it works out when a member of the New Israel 'redeems' an outcast or a foreigner into the covenant fellowship. Boaz did just this for Ruth when he 'redeemed' this young foreign woman and brought her 'home' into the fellowship of a family with a different family name (Ruth 4:5-6). This is what TI means at Isa. 56:5b.

The decision recorded at Lev. 20:24 excluded the eunuch from the covenant fellowship (cf. 21:20). But TI had now lived through a new 'moment' of revelation in God's saving plan for the world. For God had now redeemed Israel while they themselves were still unclean and while living in a foreign, and therefore unclean, land. Actually the ever-recurring sabbath day was the only institution the people had possessed that was able to hold them together — in hope — those long fifty years in exile: in hope, because the sabbath was the day of *God's* rest, after he had completed all his work (Gen. 2:1-3). That is why the sabbath remained a sign of hope to the exiles, for it taught them that God was bound, some day, to finish his work of love! The sabbath was their never-failing sacramental means of grace.

The new revelation, then, that had now come to 'unclean' Israel meant that they had to learn to *do* for the unclean foreigner (*ben-hannekar*) as much as God had done for them. Israel was to remember that 'a wandering Aramean was my father' (Deut. 26:5) ('an Amorite, and your mother a Hittite', Ezek. 16:3 adds; and see also Exod. 12:38 and Num. 11:4) so that they are as much a 'Gentile' as any other people. Then, from being a mere *ger*, a squatter, in the world of humanity, God had made them into citizens of Zion, where he had granted them an everlasting identity ('name'), that would not be 'cut off', presumably by death (cf. Isa. 55:13).

Israel is enjoined particularly to welcome 'home' the eunuch. From now on even such as he, as DI expressed the idea, was to

have as his new name 'Yahwehson', in the same way as we build
names today like Adamson or Richardson (44:5; cf. Matt. 22:41-45
and parallels). We note in consequence of this passage the Christian instinct from the beginning of the Church's story to baptize
outsiders into the new fellowship so that they might become citizens of Zion — in Acts 8:38, for example, a man who was both
a foreigner and a eunuch. What is more, though, this particular
individual, when we meet him, was reading the book of Isaiah
(vv. 30-33)!

We may draw a parallel to this situation from a statement
made by Jacob Neusner: 'It took a great effort to transform an
act of circumcision of the flesh . . . into a deepening commitment
to faith' (*First Century Judaism in Crisis*, 38). This was just where
TI helped his people to make the connection between the return
from Babylon to Zion and their own commitment to applying
the covenantal faith in their new situation. To do so, TI had first
to reinterpret Deut. 23:1-6 (we note that he was no biblical literalist!) and then proceed to pick up the thought of DI at Isa.
45:23 and develop it. TI then added into the mixture what Jeremiah had declared forcibly long before at Jer. 25:12 and 29:30-32.
Thereupon he interpreted their joint wording in the light of the
new event.

Thus when Israel began to act in the power of God's *tsedaqah*
'foreigners' would then actually ask to be allowed to 'join themselves to the Lord'. In so doing they would themselves become
'eternal', for they would now be joined to the eternal God! Such
foreigners were known in Esther's day as 'joiners' (Esth. 9:27),
even if they lived somewhere far off in the Persian Empire. All
that might be expected of them would be the keeping of the
sabbath; their doing so would motivate pagans around them to
ask about Israel's faith. Pagans, of course, kept special days as
festivals, and these were bound up with some form of religious
rites. But Israel's 'day' was not bound up with 'religion' as the
world understands the word; it was bound up with moral and
social issues that come from the very heart of God.

A group of such 'joiners' may have come over into the covenant
community from amongst any of the large numbers of foreign
peoples with whom the exiles had been forced to live when in
Babylon. Some of them perhaps were even Babylonians. (Actually, this was no new thing as we see from the names of individuals at 2 Sam. 11:3; 1 Chr. 11:39, 46.) For such, it was a

venture of faith to leave Babylon and travel in the company of Israel's invisible God to start a new life in a place where only ruins awaited them. Since Isa. 56:5 quotes directly from 55:13b, the last verse of DI's material, it would appear that such foreigners, who had not been reckoned amongst the children of Abraham (Gen. 12:1-3; 17:1-4), were in themselves a visible sign of this wholly new beginning in the story of the People of God. This beginning had, however, been foreseen by both the preexilic and the exilic prophets (Hos. 2:18-23; Jer. 31:31-34; Ezek. 36:24-28).

We would suggest that the strong faith, integrity, and loyalty of such foreigners at least contributed to arousing the people of the Covenant to hold a widened vision, in perhaps two areas. First, from now on the word 'neighbour' stretches beyond one's fellow Israelite to include all the peoples of the earth (cf. 1 Kgs. 8:41-43). Second, it taught the returned exiles to conjoin the two ideas we translate by the words 'salvation' and 'righteousness' as the one gift of God (cf. Ps. 71:15). Thus v. 8 can speak of both 'the outcasts of Israel' and of 'yet others' who are to become one with 'those already gathered'. Together, then, these component groups of God's people were being invited, in the language of the Westminster Confession, to 'glorify God and to enjoy him forever'. We note how the sentiments found in v. 7 were underlined by Jesus at John 10:16 (cf. Mark 11:17) and were embodied in Paul's argument at Rom. 12:1 when he wrote to a very mixed and multicultural congregation. We may also point to the fact that in the period of the Second Temple and after, such great scholars as Akiba, Meir, Shammai and Abtalyon were all descendants of proselytes amongst the Gentiles.

What Isaiah once had described as 'God's strange work' (Isa. 28:21-22 author's translation) had now worked a miracle. It was a 'work' that had employed, first, destruction and death and then, second, resurrection and renewal (cf. Deut. 32:39). God had worked, it seemed, not through smooth evolution but through pain and crisis, a truth that was to be repeated again and again as Israel's story was to unfold in years to come.

The basic text of our biblical faith is the Torah. But the prophets had always felt free to interpret it in the light of each new historical situation in which they found themselves (cf. Jer. 25:12). It was as if they said: 'You have heard that it was said to the men of old. . . . But I say to you . . .' (Matt. 5:21-22), whereupon the prophet would offer a *torah* of his own, but one that had of course 'evolved' from the original Torah. In the same way today the People of God have had to learn from God a new *torah* on such issues as slavery, and social and economic justice, and even on such new issues in this age of science as abortion and the use of nuclear power.

At this point, however, we see how TI's preaching takes the form of a new *torah* for the postexilic age. We can contrast his wide views with the 'fundamentalism' of Ezra some generations later. Ezra did not find TI's exegesis of Torah acceptable. But basic to TI's new *torah* is his belief that, because of a historical situation brought about by God through his 'messiah', God had now thrown open the covenant fellowship to all people of all races, nations, tongues, and moralities, along with their children (Ezek. 47:22-23). This was to be so even if they were physically deformed or, we might add today, mentally handicapped. How unlike the Greek ideal this is, in its adulation of the beauty of the human form. To be described as 'a dry tree' (Isa. 56:3) referred to a man or a woman who could not share in God's command to create children (cf. Gen. 17:15-21). In the spirit of that promise made to Sarah in Genesis, however, God himself (Isa. 56:4a) now 'gives' (v. 5) to the unmarried woman, the bachelor, the widow, the homosexual an equally valid and eschatologically significant place in the Covenant, even though these folk are unable to form a link in the historical chain of human life. The text of v. 6, as we have it in the Dead Sea Isaiah scroll, (1 QIsa) includes further wording beyond what the RSV gives us. The extra line runs: 'to become his servants (the LXX adds 'and his maidservants'!) to bless the name of Yahweh while keeping the sabbath'. Since 'keeping the sabbath' is but an incidental way of saying that a man or woman belongs in the Covenant, we can see that the Qumran community possessed a text of Isaiah that was meant for all mankind. The eunuch was not even to be an 'ordinary member' of Israel; he was to be a 'monument' (v. 5) or a pillar. It is from such a passage that we today speak of a person as being a 'pillar of the church'. Moreover, the misfit was, by grace alone, to receive a 'name', an individual identity, within the whole People of God that would render him or her, as an individual, of eternal value to God. It would appear that TI had grasped with both hands the reality and power of God's oath made and recorded at 45:23. From such a passage as this, then, we can understand how the prayer of the foreign thief at Luke 23:42 'will be accepted on my altar' (Isa. 56:7) as truly as that of any 'righteous' Israelite.

The Actual Situation (9-12)

We have heard from TI, then, that the true nature of the covenant people in their relationship to God is to be found in their calling to love and serve all mankind. But the reality was very different. Chapters 56 – 66 point to the existence of a number of parties now clustered in Jerusalem — we might even call them sects — each of whom probably believed that it alone was 'right'. These were (1) the righteous (*tsaddiqim*), (2) God's chosen ones (*anshehesed*), (3) God's servants (*'abadim*), (4) the wicked (*resha'im*), (5) the rebels (*'am sorer*), and further divisions within the community caused by disagreements on the observance or nonobservance of the Mosaic laws. And then, of course, there were various groups of pagan foreigners living right in the same street as members of each of these sects. This all means that although the 'resurrection' of Israel had now taken place, the kingdom of God certainly had not yet come!

At 1 Cor. 11:19 Paul suggests that heresies are useful, in that they force believers to take their orthodoxy seriously. Here, then, TI feels compelled to show up the sheer secularism to which some of the returnees had succumbed, the paganism and hedonism that was evidently rife amongst 'the people of the land'. After Nebuchadnezzar had ravaged Judah some Edomites had wandered in and filled the vacuum, themselves ravaging what of the city was left. Then some south Palestinians had also moved in (Ezek. 25:1 – 26:3). These had exclaimed: 'The ancient heights (*'olam*) have become our possession' (36:2). The term *'olam*, to Israel's way of thinking (though not to the Philistines and Tyrians, Moabites and Ammonites that Ezekiel mentions), really meant 'eschatologically significant'. Yet these intruders had taken over the Jerusalem heights 'with wholehearted joy and utter contempt' (vv. 5-8). TI, however, actually preaches 'good news' to those foreign settlers. He shows how God's wrath at their activities was to become the instrument of their salvation. It was to take place in two steps. Israel was first to consolidate itself before it could become God's instrument of mission. At Isa. 49:6 DI had said that the 'servant' element within Israel must first 're-store the *preserved* of Israel': preserved, held together, in the forced-labour conditions of Babylon. Only then, and second, could God fulfil his promise that 'I will give (or 'make') you to be the light of the nations, to become my salvation to the end of the earth' (rather than the wording of the RSV).

In a sermon, well-remembered by his hearers, our prophet invites the beasts of the field and of the forest to 'come to devour' (56:9) those who ought to have been the responsible leaders of the mixed population now struggling to recreate a civilized community in ruinous Jerusalem. But by so doing he was placing himself at risk. For the 'wild beasts', whatever those words mean, would not distinguish between the leadership of the various sects. These leaders had been called to be 'shepherds' (v. 11). TI uses this word in Hebrew (*ro'im*, singular *ro'eh*) as a pun upon the word 'wicked' (*ra'ah*). They 'have no understanding' of God's plan for the new nation. For them, he says, the situation had no 'meaning'. All they were interested in was their own hedonistic pleasure.

Using the language of Ezekiel (Ezek. 33:1-9) TI accuses the leadership of being watchmen who are blind to their duties (Isa. 56:10). This leadership must have included some clergy. Then TI adds a new simile of his own: the ruined city would be full of skinny dogs that foraged for and fought over any available scraps of food (v. 11). These dogs did not even have the will left to bark when a stranger approached. Such then were the people's leaders! They had lost all sense of reality, including the joy of living and of rebuilding, that is, recreating a broken society. As a result they deliberately made themselves drunk in order to drown their emptiness of spirit (v. 12). A drug such as alcohol can, of course, make one feel 'great beyond measure'.

Here then is a portrait of a society of uncouth, spiritless people. It is representative of the world at large (as seems to be the meaning behind Matt. 6:32; 10:18), a society that has no comprehension of what it means when God lets them know that they are the object of his loving purpose (Isa. 56:8). What is relevant to the present issue, however, is that such self-centred, sensuous people are even now squatting in the Holy City! Psalm 85 seems to illustrate this situation. It could have been uttered by the few faithful souls who were then wondering just what God was doing in allowing such a situation to continue.

10

CHAPTER 57

CAN THIS BE THE NEW ISRAEL?
Isaiah 57:1-21

1-2 TI now probes the eternal question, 'Why do the righteous suffer?' In doing so he digs much deeper than what is apparent in Mic. 7:2 or Ps. 12:1, for he is seeking a new *torah* on the issue. The indictment that the horrified prophet has been making in Isa. 56:9-12 against the 'watchmen' of this mixed community is expanded in this chapter to cover all elements in Jerusalem's society.

It was the great mistake of the medieval Church to give the name 'Christendom' to Europe and to accept as axiomatic that everyone born in Europe was thereby and automatically a Christian. Even though Martin Luther rebelled against this concept, in his late years, when very poor health made him despondent and pessimistic, he was grieved that in those areas of Germany which had adopted the Reformed faith there seemed to be an ever-increasing number of perverts and renegades. Similarly, it became apparent that the restored community of TI's day was not uniformly 'renewed' in faith and practice.

DI had foretold that God would lead his people out of Babylon in a new Exodus. When God had led them out of Egypt in the days of Moses, he had thereupon created them as his own people (Exod. 19:5). Now that the second Exodus had taken place, TI had to ask himself if his contemporaries were really a new people at all. He must have asked what the word 'new' in fact connoted. While in Babylon, the prophet Ezekiel had thought deeply on this issue; at Ezek. 20:32ff. he declares that this second Exodus would not be a mere physical exit from Babylon but that it would take the form of a crisis of divine judgment. [We note incidentally that Jesus interpreted his own 'exodus' — the Greek word used at Luke 9:31 — as the final outcome of this judgment of God, in

11

that through it his people would go free.] This judgment, TI believed, was now taking place. Indeed, God had now made Israel 'pass under the rod' in order that we might bring them again 'into the bond of the covenant' (Ezek. 20:37-38; cf. RSV mg). Ezekiel had realized that only in this way would Israel really become 'new'—that is, only when God had 'raised' them from their graves (37:12-13); 'raised' here translates the same verb ('*alah*) used of God's action in rescuing Israel when he brought them up out of Egypt (Exod. 32:7). Israel would then, of course, be 'new', though still continuous with the Israel of old.

But did the 'new' Israel really know that the LORD had done all of this (Ezek. 37:14)? Could Israel 'know' it so long as they remained in their sins? The prophet TI came to realize that this is not the point. The People of God are not created anew by their own faith, nor can they ever 'feel' that they are different. They are recreated by the prevenient grace and love of God (Isa. 43:1-2). The last words of the book of Ezekiel (Ezek. 48:35) affirm that when the people returned to Jerusalem they would know that the 'new' had arrived simply because 'The LORD is there'. So had he been 'there' all along with his people in the midst of their degradation and sin—but TI has more to say on this later in the chapter.

The state of affairs in Jerusalem is much worse than what was depicted at Isa. 56:9-12. The loyal Yahweh worshippers, it seems, were actually being persecuted; some were even 'disappearing'— a situation only too well known in a number of countries today. Yet even then, says TI, God was looking after his loyal covenanters and ensuring that they slept in peace.

The Courage to Speak Out (3-13)

In this rather lengthy oracle our prophet exhibits the courage of an Amos and the pictorial powers of an Isaiah. We should realize that the 'you' of v. 3 are now the great-grandchildren of the 'sons' whom Isaiah had addressed at 1:2. TI addresses such now: 'You followers of witchcraft, you brats of prostitution and whores' (one scholar's translation). While this language may reflect the frequently prophetic idiom of going 'a whoring after other gods' (Judg. 2:17 KJV), it could also be taken literally. At 56:12 the leaders had cried to each other 'Come!'. Now TI has the courage to challenge them to come and listen to God's words of judgment

addressed to them! 'Who do you think you are kidding?' or even
'taking a malicious delight in?', he asks them. 'Who are you
making faces at, putting out your tongue?—at *the living God?!*
Don't you realize that you are in a state of rebellion against "my
Covenant love" (54:10), so that you are the offspring of what
Jeremiah names as the opposite of a true vine?' (Jer. 2:21; RSV
'choice'). TI continues: 'You inflame yourselves with sexual passion by the sacred oaks (v. 5) and under every green tree'. Quite
permissibly the Targum understands 'oaks' to read 'gods', while
the LXX has taken the next step of calling these either 'no-things'
(from the Heb. *al*), or 'powers' (*el*), or 'spirits'; the Hebrew of
the OT is rich in double entendres.

Hosea, writing two centuries earlier, had described how some
Israelites had put their faith in the teachings of just such a religious sect (Hos. 2:5). Later interpreters, thinking theologically
and in the light of such a verse as Gen. 1:2, formulated the pun
mentioned above, and thus suggested that fornication is the negation of what we learn of God's purposes through his Word
(Gen. 1:3). Yet such cults were really probing mysteries like Paul
did half a millennium later when he spoke of 'principalities and
powers' (Eph. 3:10; Col. 2:15) that control our lives. Our preacher
employs first the plural in his verbs; by this means he indicts
people as separate and responsible individuals. Then at Isa. 57:6
he reverts to the feminine singular, a device by means of which
he can include all Israel as one people. God thus accuses his
bride, his spouse Israel (54:5-6), of this kind of terrible disloyalty.
Israel is the adulteress still (Ezekiel 16), even after her 'resurrection' now from the grave, and after her vindication by her God
(Isa. 56:1). Thus in TI's sermons we are constantly reminded of
Luther's famous dictum: that the Christian man is still a sinner
even though he has been redeemed.

You 'slay your children in the valleys, under the clefts of the
rocks', sacrificing your own babies to the god Molech (cf. Lev.
20:4; 2 Kgs. 23:10) in order to save your own health of mind and
soul. This is surely the most complete perversion of religious faith
(see Jer. 7:31; Mic. 6:7), for children are the gift of God. It is
our responsibility to hand on to them the Covenant, which they
in their turn are to pass on to the next generation again. But, of
course, their willingness to destroy their own children was a sign
of their deep desire for atonement with some power other than

Yahweh. They remind us of those who, neglecting their family, go in search of enlightenment and peace of mind at the feet of a guru — the ultimate selfishness that a person could commit. Or again, in those old days abortion was too dangerous for the woman's health, so society just waited for the birth. Then it appeased the gods by making the destruction of the new baby into a rite!

At v. 6 appears some other pagan cult connected with nature worship, through which offerings were made to the natural forces that had already been set aside for Yahweh. God had given Israel the Holy Land as their 'portion' (Josh. 22:25). In contrast, by their unbelief all that these pagans had as their portion was the stony bed of a dried-up wadi. Instead of possessing, as the psalmist did, the living God as his portion (Ps. 119:57; 142:5), all the sensualist had was the bitter taste in his mouth of a spent passion(17:14). In consequence of this state of affairs God himself now asks the question: 'Shall I be appeased for these things?' Again we have an echo of the First Isaiah, for at Isa. 1:10 he had declared that people living in Jerusalem were on a par with the perverted inhabitants of Sodom and Gomorrah.

At Ps. 68:16 the writer asks the high mountains of Bashan why they envy 'the mount which God desired for his abode'. Indeed, Jerusalem was often lovingly and proudly regarded as the highest mountain in the world. The true worshipper then ascended to Mt. Zion in order 'to offer sacrifice' (Isa. 57:7). However, on the day TI preached this sermon there may well have been no altar where such sacrifice could be made. Because of this it seems that some inhabitants made excursions to other nearby hilltops to sacrifice to the gods of nature, and there they practised ritual adultery to the 'powers' of sex. As psychologists have shown us in our day, the worship of nature and the worship of sex are closely related.

8 The people mentioned here were not necessarily all pagans. Some may have been from 'the people of the land' who had now become paganized. Every good Israelite knew by heart the passage known as the Shema (Deut. 6:4-9); it ends with the command to write out those words and nail them up 'on the doorposts of your house', where you can't help but see them as you go in and out. This generation, then, did not merely neglect God's command, they perverted it. The indictment of their action here means a deliberate 'out of sight, out of mind' policy. Thus when they committed adultery in their own homes they 'made a covenant' with their whores, as 1 QIsa suggests as the correct reading. This was surely a travesty of the covenant of marriage (cf. Eph. 5:21-33) and of Yahweh's covenant with Israel, which Hosea depicts in terms of marriage.

9-10 'You lavished oil on Molech' (following the reading of some of the versions). Godfrey Rolles Driver renders the passage: 'Thou wast drenched [or glistening] with oil for (= in honour of) the king' ('Difficult Words in the Hebrew Prophets', 58-59). Thus they were 'using the many kinds of ointments for which you sent off messengers to distant lands'; this action is perhaps explained by Ezek. 23:16, 40. The people had even yielded to the temptation of the cult of the dead.

This is a picture of our human propensity for doing evil. The world produces many 'go-getters' who believe they can reach any goal they choose, and then go for it no matter what the cost of their quest might be to others and, as v. 10 implies, whether there be a God or not. On the other hand, the sentence may mean that the sexual potency of these 'worshippers' never seemed to be exhausted. TI knows well Leviticus 20, with its prohibition of all sexual perversions.

11-13 So our prophet, in his sermon to the mixed crowd before him, asks of what god they are now in dread. The result of their worship will be that they will be living a lie, for a personal lie is always a lie against God. Especially is this so of any form of syncretistic 'goodness'. It is what Plato would call 'the lie in the soul'. So why had they run away from the divine Lover?

The popular idea is that in the biblical witness concerning God the emphasis is upon God's omnipotence. But that is a great mistake, for what we meet with is rather God's impotence! We see in the Bible how humanity has taken the initiative away from God thus leaving him 'defenceless', and how God then submits himself to the freedom, to the initiative, to the reaction of his creature man. The Isaian tradition, we find, directs people throughout to God's powerlessness and God's suffering, for it is only the suffering God who can help. And so we find that it is

God's defencelessness that is in fact the revelation of his power
and of his superiority to sinful mankind (v. 18). Consequently,
God is never absent from his people, despite the cry at 64:1. God
is present even in his judgments, always waiting to 'heal him
. . . and requite him with comfort' (57:18).

How patient I am, says TI for Israel's God, holding my peace
at your behaviour (cf. 42:14). But now, I myself will make a
report on your idea of love (not 'righteousness', as RSV, in the
modern, popular sense of the term, but 'compassionate love', as
we saw in ch. 56). 'I will tell of your doings', but this will not be
to your advantage. When you cry for help, just see if your collection of gods (or, with 1 QIsa, 'those who gather you', like ripe
fruit) will 'deliver' you (v. 13). Note that the word 'deliver' (*hitsil*)
means only to rescue; when God rescues, on the other hand, he
also saves (*hoshia'*), which therefore covers both rescuing from
evil and saving from the power of sin.

The New Community (14-21)

A new 'sermonette' begins here. Till now God has addressed the
people in the feminine singular, so that 'she' refers to Zion, or to
those who are living in the city. But in this address he speaks to
the people in the plural, as 'you', and so to each individual in
turn. The 'people' now, however, are clearly only the faithful
amongst Israel. As 43:1-7 had shown, these are God's own forgiven sinners, whether they were returnees from Babylon or
members of the *'am ha-arets,* the people of the land who had never
been in exile.

Verse 14 embodies the same instructions as 40:3-5, which was
uttered before the new Exodus from Babylon had taken place.
But now that 'my people' were back at 'home', they needed to
be reminded that their home was first of all the home of the One
'whose name is Holy'! Despite that reality, they were being invited into it even as the father welcomes in his prodigal son.
Although Zion was 'the highest of the mountains', in a pictorial
theological sense (2:2), First Isaiah had declared: 'How the faithful city has become a harlot!' (1:21). Yet it was from that situation
that Isaiah had raised his eyes to the vision he gives us of the
city in ch. 2, a vision now about to be confirmed. This had happened through the forgiveness and mercy of God alone (1:18)
who, as TI declares, had 'emptied himself' (cf. Phil. 2:7) in order

to 'dwell' with one who is himself 'fallen' in spirit, with one who cannot now descend any lower than he is (Isa. 57:15).

The prophets normally declare 'Thus has the LORD said' (rather than the RSV rendering 'Thus says the LORD'). By this means they show that what God is saying through them is part of the revelation already recorded in the Torah. But TI's phrase 'And it shall be said' (which he substitutes for the 'voice' crying at 40:3) is a wholly new way of speaking. By it he shows that, under God, his *torah* is a new deduction culled rather from history — that is, from the revelation of God's love in Israel's story — and not from the Torah. Israel was that nation called 'sons of the sorceress' (57:3) who by grace alone are now addressed as 'my people'. God is the Creator and Re-creator, as DI had affirmed some sixteen times. In the beginning God had created man by breathing 'into his nostrils the breath of life' (Gen. 2:7). Now he had 'come down' in order to dwell with humble human beings, 'to revive the spirit of the humble' by breathing new life into them (cf. Ps. 34:18). What a God this is, then, of whom our preacher proclaims in the midst of the ruins of the city and amongst the broken personalities of that city's inhabitants. For to 'revive the heart' means to recreate the seat of the personality so as to receive a new nature, so as to become a new person.

Patterning his message on that of his predecessors, TI uses the name 'Holy One of Israel', first used for the Divine Being by Isaiah of Jerusalem (e.g., 1:4; see also 60:9). The Targum adds here to the RSV's 'high and lofty One', who dwells 'with him who is of a contrite and humble spirit', the words 'in his Shekinah'. This is the technical term used by the scribes to mean God's 'dwelling-place', as the meaning of this Hebrew word had developed by NT times. John uses this same term in his statement, 'the Word *dwelt* among us' (John 1:14); he employed it both because it was compatible with the language of Isaiah and because 'dwell' in Greek (*skenoo*) features the same consonants as the Hebrew root (*sh-k-n*) underlying Shekinah. At Isa. 45:14 we read that God was 'in' (not 'with', as RSV) Israel when, as the Suffering Servant, Israel was reduced to the lowest level of existence (53:1-9) and thereafter when 'he poured out his soul to death' (v. 12). Is it any wonder that Jesus quoted 'Isaiah' so frequently, since the Master, a Hebrew speaker, would recognize the meaning of this prophetic name of God?

16 This is truly preaching with insight. God is justified in his wrath, else he would be neither the God of justice nor the God of love, neither the God for us nor the God against us. For love does not turn its eyes away from evil or hide itself from sin. Nor would the God of love ever expect us to say what some evangelists think is a biblical view: 'God loves you, but hates your sin'. Such thinking is a 'hangover' from the 'Greek' world of thought that separated body and soul from each other. There is no such thing as sin in itself; there are only sinners. The young Isaiah suffered the judgment of God's hatred and underwent the cauterization of God's judgment upon his own body when the burning coal touched him, coming as it did from the very heart of God himself (6:6-7). It was only then that he could know the forgiveness and renewal of God.

17 Yet God's justifiable wrath is not unending (54:7-8), even though Israel's rebellious stance seemed to be (Col. 3:5 seems to quote this verse). At this point TI picks upon God's horror of 'covetousness' (*betsa'*). This is a strong word in Hebrew. It describes lustful acts of violence with the purpose of dominating another's personality in order to achieve one's purpose at any price. We observe the growth of this particular sin in our day as everywhere there seems to be a build-up of violence. TI does not declare such an outlook on life to be merely immoral, that is, as belonging to the second half of the Ten Commandments. He condemns it as a breaking of the First Commandment, for one who acts in this way is an idolator. DI had some years before shown that idolatry goes far beyond the mere whittling of a wooden idol out of a tree stump (Isa. 44:9-20). Idolatry is the setting up of one's own ego with all its lustful passions against the creative and loving will of God, and so is an egotistical drive for the attainment of one's goal at any price. Consequently this word *betsa'* covers such acts as rape, violent crime, 'wheeler-dealer' activities, 'my country right or wrong', expropriation of the weak, making war to enlarge one's boundary, and so on. In his last chapter TI deals with the significance of such behaviour in the light of God's saving love.

18 So then, just because Israel's spirit is weak (even 'swooning', *ya'atoph*) in my presence (rather than the RSV rendering of v. 16)

18

says God, I seize the opportunity to show him grace! 'I have seen his ways'; just because of that, 'I will heal him' and comfort him. So God is the Good Physician in a manner and to a degree unknown outside the Scriptures. For God uses our sins as occasions for the outpouring of his grace. To 'requite' in English seems something like 'to pay back'. The Hebrew, however, means 'But I will fill him full with comfort' — I will pay him back with love! DI's first words had been such (40:1) where this word 'comfort' (*niham*) occurs. Its author at that point called himself merely 'a voice' (v. 6), so self-effacing was he. Yet aware as he was of his responsibility to interpret the purposes of God to his generation, he later dared to call himself also a *melits* (43:27), which can be best translated as 'interpreter'. In revealing God's self-effacement, therefore, in this self-effacing way, the whole book of Isaiah is declaring that God's transcendence is to be understood by knowing his immanence, hidden as it is in Israel. Yet what is amazing to us now is that this self-effacing God actually takes the initiative. For at 57:18 we hear him saying 'I will lead . . . I will requite . . . I am creating'.

DI had repeatedly called God the Creator, employing the active participle of the verb to do so, thus meaning 'the Creating One'. But here God's act is one specifically of *re*-creating: 'For those who are at present filled, not with comfort, but with self-loathing I will create "fruit for their lips" '; that is, 'I will give them words to speak constructively to their neighbours, words that will produce in others integrity of mind and heart'.

19 Their theme will be *shalom, shalom,* both to those now in Jerusalem ('the near') and to those not yet returned from Babylon ('the far'), and in this way 'I will heal them'. Heal whom? The answer must be those who speak *tsedaqah*, words of creative love. In fact, TI is saying virtually 'Blessed are those who mourn, for they shall be comforted, even as I give them the words with which they may comfort others, and so, in this way, heal them in their turn'.

Bara ('create') and *shalom* ('peace') are both terms that accompany God's purpose of redemption in and through his covenant people. We have asked the question, with TI, 'Can this be the New Israel?' Now we see that the answer can only be 'yes'. It was, in fact, this generation that was now back in Jerusalem simply because it was the forgiven and renewed Israel; '*Because of* his iniquity . . . I will heal him'. What a great expression of the good news of God this is, one that must be true forever, simply because God is the same forever. We note that the NT never speaks of the Church as the New Israel, for its writers were aware that in preceding days God had never broken his Covenant with his own chosen people (Rom. 11:1-5). But since the greater part of the Israel of Paul's day had become hardened against the view that their election was for the salvation of the Gentiles, God had had to act again to re-create, and so to fulfil his plan, by using their trespass to bring salvation, not just to the covenant people themselves but also to the Gentiles (v. 11). There have been periods in history when the Church has emphasised God's redemptive love over against his recreative activity. But, as the whole book of Isaiah reminds us, there is really no dichotomy here, for redemption is in fact another term for re-creation. This theme is renewed at Isa. 65:17-18.

Shalom is the end-product of God's creative activity. The root of the noun implies fulness (cf. v. 18), wholeness, completion, in a general sense. But insofar as human beings can understand the word, it speaks of deep satisfaction, of warm and loving coop- eration between family and family, nation and nation, and the harmonious functioning of all aspects of the natural world. In this sense it had occurred as an element in the covenantal prom- ises of God (Num. 25:12; Isa. 54:10; Ezek. 34:25; 37:26). Embed- ded in the book of Isaiah is a narrative taken from 2 Kgs. (Isaiah 36 – 39), where we read that King Hezekiah fell sick. God then restored him with a promise of more life for a limited period (38:1-8). But a limited period was not enough for Hezekiah. What he sought for was full salvation from both sin and death (vv. 10-18). His response in song to God's action thus becomes an Isaian liturgy that expresses the faith that, as Creator, God is also the Re-creator of all, and so brings the *shalom* that is his own Being into the life of Israel. The 'fruit of the lips' therefore is the expression in words, from the mouth of a renewed person- ality, of the *shalom* which the latter has received and is now seek- ing to extend to his neighbour.

In Paul's day Jews could enter the inner court of the temple, but all others had to stay outside. Thus at Eph. 2:13 Paul em- ploys these words of TI to speak to his own generation, when he sees the 'near', the Jewish people, and the 'far', the Gentiles, all assembling together in the inner court.

20-21 In contrast to this marvellous 'gospel', the wicked, says TI, spend their days in chaos, the *tohu* of Gen. 1:2. We recall that throughout both the OT and the NT the darkness that represents the state of rebellion against the revealed Light is to be found lying over the chaotic waters of the primal deep, *tehom* (see Jude 13). That is why 'there is no peace, says my God, for the wicked'. *Shalom*, then, is to be found, not through political action, but in God's gracious promise and the gift of his healing power to *all* mankind.

TRUE RELIGION
Isaiah 58:1-14

1-3b Chapter 58 contains a timeless sermon. It is such because it is the Word of God to our author, as it were, and God's Word does not change. Yet it was spoken to a particular situation, and to a particular group of self-righteous people amongst the returned exiles who must have been a thorn in TI's flesh. This was because they believed themselves to be 'holier' than the ordinary folk and so would take it for granted that they were the leaders of this, a 'religious' community within the People of God. Although this 'Word of the LORD' here has been available in written form to all later generations, many 'righteous' leaders of the People of God seem to have been unimpressed by it. For example there was the high priest Jason (2 Macc. 4:25) who possessed 'no qualification for the high priesthood, but having the hot temper of a cruel tyrant and the rage of a savage wild beast' — not to speak of various popes and inquisitors in later medieval Europe.

The concrete situation addressed was the calling of a day of fasting and lamentation. Under the circumstances such was a perversion of God's will; consequently TI had to 'declare to my people their transgression' (actually 'rebellion'). We should remember that, in the Semitic way of speaking, 'fasting' meant more than refraining from eating. The word stood for all that was implied in a self-righteous religiosity that divorced faith from love. (A good illustration of this point is that the decision by the civic authorities to allow people to eat sausage during the Lenten fast was the signal for the Reformation to break out in Zurich.) TI is not preaching now to the flagrantly wicked nor to the idolators amongst the new settlers; rather, he is addressing certain individuals amongst the returned exiles themselves, as the Hebrew shows. These people, to use today's language, rejoiced to declare that they had been 'saved'; whereas, TI declares, no person is saved till he loves his neighbour even as God has loved him. This group sought to show their joy in the LORD by meticulous observance of public worship — 'they delight to know my ways'. By the year 536, it would seem, an altar of some kind had been re-erected where the old altar had stood; around it this pious group would assemble for the public worship of God. It was to this group, then, sure of their own probity, that TI was to 'cry aloud, spare not' (that is, *'without pause'*), 'lift up your voice like a trumpet', for a trumpet was used as an alarm to announce the approach of an enemy.

What had gone wrong between God and these pious believers? It was that they had broken (*pasha'*) their side of the Covenant that God had given them as his gracious gift. By their introspective religiosity they had failed to allow God to use them for his plan of world redemption. Such, says v. 1d is their 'sin' (*hattath*), the 'missing the mark' of their high calling! It was as if there had been no Isaiah before them, no prophet to interpret the meaning of servanthood, no Ezekiel to describe what it means for Israel to be born again. In the mind of this pious group God's saving plan had stopped with them. That was why, therefore, they could not understand why God was paying no attention to their fasts and to their other meticulously ordered practices. This group actually answered God back to his face.

3c-5 'Behold' is the first word God uses to reply to them, meaning 'Open your eyes, think, see!' Your religious practices are expressions of your basic egotism; you are enjoying yourself in affirming your own self-righteousness, but you are not giving me joy. 'They delight to draw near to God', to deepen their own spiritual life (rather than RSV mg at v. 3d; cf. Luke 9:23-24).

Two terms in this sentence are important theologically and also play upon each other. The first of these words, 'day', does not refer to a twenty-four-hour period. It points rather to the idea of an eschatological 'moment', being used much as is the word *kairos* in the NT (cf. Mark 13:33). Certain moments, certain deeds, certain places have significance for all eternity. The temple was such a place; but since in TI's day it lay in ruins, people had lost their former awareness of that building as a place of mystical and cosmic importance in which heaven, the earth and the un-

derworld, the beginning of time, the present and the end, Israel
and the nations, all coalesced. So with the Torah. God's Word
therein spoke more than ethical obedience; it involved acceptance
through faith of the whole divine plan of salvation. *Doing* it was
a condition of remaining within the covenant community (v. 5;
cf. Matt. 7:21), not rejoicing in one's own salvation; otherwise
God would not respond with the words, 'Here I am' (v. 9). We
are to note that ritualistic fasting is not in itself commanded in
the Torah. Lev. 16:29, 31 deals only with humbling oneself and
not with abstaining from food. The New Israel does not now
need to fast any more than do Jesus' disciples, in that, for them
the Bridegroom had come (Isa. 54:1-17; Matt. 9:14-15); they
were now a forgiven people. There was danger, however, in TI's
position. It might appear to some that he was objecting to the
established cult that clearly helped simple people to control their
religious life. Many scholars believe that the secret of the success
(or the danger!) of the Reformation was its replacing the traditional sacramental community and authority of the Church with
the narrow, subjective feelings of individuals. This could, in some
cases, lead to an approval of religious indifference, moral indis-
cipline, and rebelliousness (S. Ozment, *The Age of Reform 1250-1550*,
210). Perhaps the situation is repeating itself today in modern
Western Christendom.

Then there is the word *hephets*. It can indeed mean 'pleasure',
but it occurs in DI in another sense, well-known of course to our
author. There it refers to God's purpose, will, or plan (e.g., 53:10)
that is to work out through the Servant. This is the sense it bears
also throughout the long Ps. 119. Here, then, what this sermon
declares is that by one's conscious decision to fast, that is, to be
'religious', he is following his own selfishly thought-out plan for
his life, not God's. The person is abandoning what ch. 56 had to
say about the relationship between *tsedaqah* and *tsedeq*, and how
the 'feminine activity' must (as in the Golden Rule) follow God's
action described by the masculine term. And since God's action
has eternal significance, then its consequential action by mankind
must also (cf. Matt. 12:36; 25:31-46). 'Is such the fast that I
(God) choose?' Your choice conflicts with what is 'my' *hephets*,
that is, what is 'acceptable to the LORD'. This is made evident
in the event. For in fasting one gets hungry, and as a result gets
bad-tempered and quarrelsome. That is the very opposite of fast-

ing as a means of mortifying oneself with the object of examining one's sinful ways.

The dichotomy between God's *hephets* and mankind's *hephets* is even more distinct. Instead of approaching their workers in a spirit of *tsedaqah*, some amongst the returned exiles treated them abominably, actually even oppressing them with physical violence. These workers would be the simple, uneducated 'People of the Land', quite unlike some of the well-to-do returnees (cf. Ezra 1:6). Those unskilled labourers were probably being employed now to build homes for the prosperous priests and leaders (Hag. 1:4-6). In a word, then, the fasting of hypocrites is an abomination to the LORD. True fasting must be motivated by repentance and love.

God's Thunderous Reply (6-7)

In a word, God's answer to the self-righteous, religious element is — 'Love!' God's chosen fast is:

(a) 'To loose the bonds of wickedness, to undo the thongs of the yoke', or, as the LXX translates it, 'to untie the knots of hard bargains'. This was God's act of *tsedeq* when he freed the exiles from the evil yoke of Babylon. Israel was then meant to respond in the same spirit, by acts of *tsedaqah* — by putting an end to man's inhumanity to man, the exploitation of the poor by the rich, of poor nations by sophisticated economies.

(b) The divine demand for social justice is repeated: 'to let the oppressed go free, and to break every yoke', as God had delivered Israel from Egypt. God created mankind to be free, and here he demands that all people receive this, their divinely ordained heritage.

At this point we make two comments. (1) It is tragic that even today, when the Bible is an open book for all to read, millions of churchgoers have not yet grasped that the biblical faith is not concerned primarily with the saving of one's own individual soul. (2) The divine command here is virtually an enlargement upon what is expressed succinctly at 61:1, a passage upon which Jesus set his seal when he declared that this divine command had now been fulfilled in himself (Luke 4:18-21).

(c) 'To share your bread with the hungry'. The standard of living of the peasants squatting in and around Jerusalem must have been abysmally low. The richer, educated, and more cul-

tured element in the community (the 'upper classes') were not
to act towards these poor like the proverbial lady-bountiful of the
Victorian era. To 'share' (*paras*) is literally to 'break in two', to
give the poor half of what one has. Martin Luther permitted
religion to be identified with neither ethics nor social justice for,
he believed, it transcended both. In line with TI he taught that
acts of *tsedaqah* revealed the transcendental nature of the faith,
the *tsedeq* of God.

(d) What then does this word 'share' mean by going half and
half? One is to 'bring the homeless poor', the refugee, the displaced person, 'into your house' (cf. Deut. 14:29). He will then
occupy one half of it! An important reality to note is that to be
homeless is to be rootless. In that state one no longer feels part
of human society. Israel in exile had experienced such depriva-
tion: God had now restored them to their homeland, where they
could put down roots again. Israel was therefore to share this
compassionate gift of God with others.

(e) To clothe 'the naked' by reducing one's own wardrobe.
This command of God has no negatives in it. Some people today
suppose that one must not do this and not do that to be amongst
the 'faithful'. But God's words are all positive commands to perform acts of love, compassion, and care for all his 'poor', whoever
they are, and wherever they may be (cf. Matt. 25:31-46).

From the Talmud (*Ned.* 40) we learn: 'He who visits the sick
will be saved from the judgment of Gehinnom'. Speaking generally, to the rabbis kindness was 'higher' than almsgiving. Thus
at Mishnah *Aboth* i.2 we read: 'On three things the world stands,
on Torah, worship, and performances of kindness'. In his masterly
survey of European thought and culture, *Civilisation,* Lord Ken-
neth Clark points to the fact that it was only towards the end of
the Victorian era, after writers such as Charles Dickens and art-
ists like William Hogarth had shown up the horrible conditions
of the poor in, for example, London's East End, that we could
call that period 'The Dawn of the Age of Kindness'. Self-denial,
as in fasting, without love does nothing to advance God's *hephets*
for his world. OT scholars for a century now have sought to show
the Church — which, in many areas, has consistently refused to
accept their findings — that the OT 'secularized religion'. It may
be that God has had to use the figure of Karl Marx in this century
to open the eyes of believers, just as he used the figure of the

pagan King Cyrus to effect the release of TI's generation from the bondage of a selfish cult.

(f) There is a surprising addition to this command of God at v. 7d. One is 'not to hide yourself from your own flesh'. Deut. 22:1, 3-4 speaks of the evil of pretending not to 'see your brother's ox or his sheep go astray', and thus to avoid having to help him bring them back; and so with any of 'your brother's' property that he has lost. How much more, then, does this *torah* apply in the case of one's own family. There is the philanthropist who donates large sums to charity but at home can be mean and even cruel to his wife and children. The modern science of psychology has made it clear that children become antisocial and turn to violent ways when their parents 'hide themselves', that is, do not shower love and affection upon them. Not only do these children then find themselves unloved, they come to believe that they are unlovable.

True Spirituality (8-9a)

There are always those who work hard to become spiritually minded. They suppose that God expects us to search for holiness, as is the case in Hinduism. But this is not true of the OT. Such a search for holiness implies an individualistic and selfish view of our relationship with God. As Jesus put it, 'He who finds his life (the fulfilment of his personality or spiritual union with God) will lose it'. Then he adds, 'and he who loses his life (his spiritual union with God) for my sake will find it' (Matt. 10:39). TI understands that true spirituality shines forth from the face of him who does what God does (as at Exod. 34:29) and who therefore talks with God even as he pours himself out for others.

This idea is now expressed in terms of light, even as God himself is Light, as TI remembers the Word uttered at Isa. 49:6: 'I will give you as a light to the nations'. So TI continues by declaring that only when one does what God does 'shall your light break forth like the dawn', as when the rising sun splits the night sky to bring hope and joy to a world that is sitting in darkness. Then too 'your healing (of others, not of your own soul) shall spring up speedily', as a medicinal plant that can be used immediately to heal a dangerous wound. This is, of course, the kind of acted prayer that 'the LORD will answer', because it reveals not a selfish desire for one's own good but an unselfish

27

desire to love the needy even as God has loved us. In the very act of sharing bread with the hungry, therefore, God 'will say, Here I am'; for he himself has become the Real Presence in the act of the breaking of bread. Then 'your righteousness (God's word, *tsedeq*, this time!) shall go before you'. What theological depths we discover in TI's careful use of his two terms for righteousness! And 'the glory of the LORD', not human glory (this word is used in parallel with *tsedeq*), will bring up the rear, thus crowning a person's loving actions with his own unspeakable glory.

9b-12 TI now considers this divine declaration in detail. To 'take away the yoke' means to break forcefully the weighty cross-bar that greedy, vicious, and powerful people have continually laid upon the backs of simple folk, including in their number even little children. As Fyodor Dostoevsky wrote in *The Brothers Karamazov*: 'It is the defencelessness of children that tempts the tormentor, that sets his vile blood on fire'. So it was with the 'warders' of Auschwitz, both male and female, as they relentlessly prodded their naked captives into the gas ovens.

'The pointing of the finger' was an act of contempt, employed when the 'snob' mentioned above used the issue of a class barrier to hold himself aloof. But, TI continues, 'if you pour yourself out for the hungry' (the verb used of the Suffering Servant at 53:12 and of the eternal Christ at Phil. 2:7), then your election within the Covenant to be God's instrument will be justified. But there is more to it than that one should be obedient. One's concern for the afflicted must be to satisfy that other person's desire, or fulfil his personality, before considering oneself.

In passing we note how the world only too often misunderstands this passage. For there are social workers of good will who do not rely upon God's promises; these may then merely drop a case of human misery and go home when the clock strikes the end of the working day. TI says, on the other hand, that God's kind of servant, who knows what it means to pour himself out for others, cannot let his client go until he leads him to peace. Then he goes home on a 'high' of joy, that deep satisfaction known to the Suffering Servant (53:11), whose creative nature is described again at 61:4. This creativity is of God. He does this for a person by 'steeling his bones', as if by putting them in iron splints.

TI recognizes here the true balance that Augustine adduces in his *City of God* (xix. 19): 'No man has a right to lead such a life of contemplation as to forget in his own ease the service due to his neighbour; nor has any man a right to be so immersed in active life as to neglect the contemplation of God'. From another angle, if only a priest had known his 'Isaiah' and been able to introduce King Henry VII of England to this chapter, that king would not have ordered ten thousand masses for his soul at six-pence each. Full, unconditional forgiveness of sin and assurance of salvation were utterly foreign concepts to medieval theology and religious practice.

As with 'a watered garden', fruit, flowers, and vegetables show their strength and beauty when God supplies the garden with a perennial spring. In the case of rebuilding the city the emphasis is upon God and mankind working together, yet only when and if mankind follows the ideal plan that comes from the mind of God himself.

An Appendix on the Sabbath (13-14)

The sabbath is a gift to Israel from the holy God, so it too is holy (Exod. 16:23). Thus it is not to be trampled upon (cf. 3:5), treated as a mere secular holiday. It is not to be a day when one chooses to do one's 'own thing' (*hephets*), unrelated to God's *hephets*, his purpose, his plan, his will. Rather, 'if you call the sabbath a delight ... you shall take delight in the LORD' of the sabbath. In doing so one shall find the deepest of all satisfactions, nay, the very highest, as if he or she were riding 'upon the heights of the earth'. The joy of the sabbath is thus expressed by TI when he quotes from his 'sourcebook', Deut. 32:13. For there we read, 'He made him stride (rather than 'ride') on the high places of the earth' in exultation, exuberance, and gratitude. These heights are where God places his feet, so from there one in his turn will be able to view the world below lying in the hands of God (cf. Matt. 4:8). This 'holy' land that the faithful will see, he continues, Yahweh has long promised to Israel's 'father', Jacob, to remain as the heritage of Jacob's children's children. Finally, as TI puts it, it is as if the LORD had signed this oracle himself, although not by hand, for his word alone is enough.

Every religion must possess a minimum of formal observance, for human beings cannot live by the spirit alone. To try to do so is like playing a game of football without rules. The regulations around sabbath observance might, and certainly did, vary from generation to generation. For one thing, it must have been well-nigh impossible to observe the day at all in Babylon, a land where all people had to work seven days a week. And certainly the minutiae of observance apparent in NT times were unknown in TI's day. But TI's contemporaries saw the missionary value of sabbath keeping when the pagans squatting in Jerusalem asked such questions as 'Where is your God, Yahweh?' 'How do you know it was he, your invisible God, who brought you home to Zion?' God himself had given Israel the required answer to such questions. It was to 'call the sabbath a delight'. It was as the well-known opening to the Westminster Catechism has put it in immortal words: 'Man's chief end is to glorify God and to enjoy him forever'.

CHAPTER 59

SIN SEPARATES MANKIND FROM GOD
Isaiah 59:1-21

This chapter is difficult both to place and to date. As a sermon it is a unity. Yet it is not necessarily from the same mouth as the sermon in ch. 58. The preacher may be referring to one of two situations.

(a) In the face of the very unsettling conditions confronting the returned Israelites, he may have felt it necessary to sound a warning note. So in this passage, expressed in verse like most of the other oracles we are reading, he may be describing the kind of rebellious life Israel had been leading in the days of Jeremiah a century before. Their conduct at that time had brought about God's judgment upon his people. As Jeremiah had put it, God had seen fit to summon 'his servant Nebuchadnezzar' to act on his behalf and so to bring about the exile of God's people to Babylon.

(b) The second possibility is that this preacher is confronting his contemporaries with their actual behaviour at the moment. Probably some years have now passed. The date for the occasion of this sermon is now, let us say, 525 B.C. The first flush of enthusiasm and idealism has now passed — a decade can see a complete change of mood in a people or nation. Consequently, in reaction to the enormous problem of recreating in Jerusalem a civilized community — from scratch, so to speak, almost even from the level of primitive society without any tools — men and women had been reverting to dishonest ways, brutality, and injustice. Actually, to crown their vexation and exasperation they had been afflicted with a series of poor harvests (Hag. 1:6). Thus they did not have enough to eat nor sufficient wool to clothe their backs, and inflation had made holes in the value of money. Such

31

is the situation when a city, in all ages, has been ravaged, burnt, and — today — bombed (cf. Isa. 3:1-5). So the kind of 'man's inhumanity to man' that we have seen in our lifetime can illuminate the chaotic moral and spiritual situation of TI's day. To do so is to take the Bible seriously, and not to sentimentalize the reaction of the people then, just because they were the 'People of God'. As such, they were a forgiven people, but, as Martin Luther liked to reiterate, they were still sinners, just as were the members of the church at Corinth to whom Paul had preached the gospel.

One thing, however, is sure. The people preached to here are not the 'Samaritans' we hear of a century later in Nehemiah.

1-8 This first half of the sermon is a reproach. The speaker begins, most wisely, not with mankind and their weaknesses, but with God and his strength. For the returned settlers had lost confidence in this divine strength. So he declares that it was the sin of each individual in the community (the verbs and nouns here are in the plural) which had only made it appear that God had lost his hold upon them. It was in fact 'your iniquities' that 'have made a separation between you and your God'.

It is always man, mankind, who alienates himself from God, not God from man. At the first God made man free — in his image, for God is free — free to make his own choices; whereupon man used his freedom to shake himself free of God. So it is that, since sin is repugnant to God's holiness, God must necessarily turn his face from the source of sin, the sinner. The only way, then, through the impasse, the separation, that has transpired is for God to take the initiative once again and to reach out to the sinner across the divide in forgiving love. This he has always obviously been able to do, for 'the LORD'S hand is not shortened, that it cannot save'. We are shown that the 'separation' is not between 'matter' and 'spirit', as in pagan thought, or between 'this world' and 'the world to come'; it is between fellowship with God and alienation from him through sin. We noted when we read 56:3 that there is no 'natural' division between race and race, colour and colour, homosexuality and heterosexuality; and we noted that this word 'separation' (*hibdil*) is rooted as far back as Gen. 1:4. There God separates between light and darkness, and so sets the scene for his continuing war against the darkness of evil and sin.

Being an accomplished public speaker, our preacher begins with the Hebrew word *hen* (more commonly found in the form *hinneh*). Translated as 'Behold!' this word can lose meaning for us — as can its Greek equivalent, *idou*, when we hear it from the lips of Jesus — if we ignore the Semitic way of expressing reality. The word invites us to think, not in terms of scientific accuracy, but by using our poetic imagination, to see with the inner eye, to have a mental picture, in this case, of what separation entails. How else dare a human being suggest, unless in this picture form and in fun, that God might have one arm shorter than the other!? Or that divine grace is really only cheap grace?

Our preacher quotes his master, DI, who at 50:2 uses this phrase about God's arm being too short, and then proceeds to show how, so far from being helpless, God had stooped to overcome the separation by acting through his Suffering Servant, Israel. Perhaps this sermon was delivered at a solemn assembly such as a celebration of New Year. Again, the preacher may have used Ps. 89:13 as his text: 'Thou hast a mighty arm; strong is thy hand, high thy right hand'.

At that time, he explains, God had redeemed his people by acting from 'within', as it were, not merely from 'on high', and not by annihilating the separation but by making himself one with sinful Israel in their 'death-and-resurrection' experience. (See the discussion of this issue at Isa. 45:14-15 in the volume *Servant Theology* in this series). Thus, no matter how far Israel had fallen from grace, God was still with that people as their loving 'Spouse'.

We cannot blame Israel for disloyalty to their Saviour God. The Israel of that day had very naturally supposed that when God fulfilled his promise to bring Israel 'home' the kingdom of God would then arrive, 'paradise' would follow the Exile, real *shalom* would finally eventuate. We cannot blame them, for the early Church did just the same, and various adventist groups have persisted to this day in the same hope. It was the hope that with the resurrection of Jesus the Second Coming was bound to follow, even 'the end of the world'.

Humanity needs a concept of peace, a vision of *shalom* which it can then pursue. The concept is a pragmatic one; the vision, however, is eschatological. But the two are the two sides of a coin. Thus the revelation which the OT gives us is that grace and love are not optional extras in the life of the world, but are absolutely indispensable to human existence.

In what follows the fact of the divisions in the society of TI's day, which are at odds with each other, is well brought out in the preacher's choice of terms 'your', 'they', 'we', 'his'. 'Your twisted wickednesses have been separating (on and on) between you and your God (author's translation)'; 'your guilt has continued to alienate you from your Covenant Partner, and your sins have hid "Face" from you', the word 'Face' being used as if it were another name for God. TI had clearly absorbed the significance of such a passage as Exod. 33:14 which reads: 'My "face" (RSV 'presence') will go with you, and I will give you rest'.

'Blood' (v. 3) means economic pressure upon the poor, not murder (1:15). 'Justly', 'goes to law', 'honestly' (59:4) are all words that apply in the first place to the divine nature and activity. For example, *emunah* ('honestly') is really 'truth'. Truth is not a thing in itself, as Pilate, at John 18:38, seemed to believe. Truth is something that happens between two or more persons, for it has to do with relationships. It is not to be sought in the tranquil spirit of the believer, but rather in action, in the conquest of evil, in the fruit of the true knowledge of God (H. Wildberger, *Jesaja*, 461). It is here therefore that the concept of the Word acquires its full significance. God himself is a 'community', for he is *elohim*, a plural word. But Israel, though united by grace with God through the Covenant, had contaminated that reality about the God who had bound himself to them.

'Empty pleas' is the word *tohu*, that chaos which was there in the beginning (Gen. 1:2), that darkness which, as we have newly noted, God had separated from the light. So we are led far beyond what our RSV translation conveys. What we have is, 'They put their trust in', 'they bet their life upon *tohu*', and 'they speak *sheqer*', that contempt for the truth which is the mark of a perverted soul. Ulrich E. Simon illustrates this horror in the words: 'The victims of Auschwitz died because pagan madness wished to extirpate the light and to rule the world in dark, ecstatic nihilism' (*A Theology of Auschwitz*, 88).

'Lies' is *shaw*, the 'perversion' referred to in the Third Commandment (Exod. 20:7); this verse virtually quotes Job 15:35. Paul had to face this issue also in the early Church (Acts 13:10). Again, fancy sitting on eggs that hatch out as venomous snakes

(Isa. 59:5), or, as the line before puts it, 'they enter into a wretched pregnancy that issues in iniquity (author's translation)', meaning that instead of being able to create life in the womb they can only create death (cf. Gen. 3:15). Once again, then, our preacher has drawn upon his 'sourcebook', the Song of Moses, at Deut. 32:33; and to show that this is no strange new theology of his own, he seems also to be quoting from a collection of proverbs with which his audience would be acquainted. In a word, what he is saying is that everything they are doing is negative, *shaw*, *tohu*, the opposite of all the activities listed in ch. 58 that lead to the *shalom* of God. 'He who eats their eggs dies'; that is, he who joins up with their sect goes down to 'hell'.

9-15a These verses constitute a group confession. To understand the declaration that follows we must first discover the situation to which it was addressed, else it makes little sense. Our imagination must be stirred to grasp the immensity of the logistics required by the huge migration of fifty thousand persons in all who returned from Babylon (Ezra 2). They had to be 'tented', fed, watered, doctored, clothed throughout the long, perhaps six-month march. They had set off with the express permission of Cyrus king of the Persian Empire so that the 'Return' was in no sense a deportation. Only the first detachments of this huge 'army of the Lord', as we have suggested before, would by now have reached their goal. But these would probably have comprised largely the young and the eager, youthful enthusiasts who undertook to get there first and prepare for the reception of the slower detachments of women and children and of all the accoutrements of the temple that Cyrus had expressly returned to their rightful owners. Had they travelled swiftly and with light hearts, 'singing the songs of Zion' as they went, and quoting to each other snatches of the sermons of DI which they had heard him preach in Babylon? But when they arrived, there was no one there to help them recreate their lives in the ruins of the Holy City. There was only hostility.

Some bold spirit, therefore, puts his finger upon the spiritual malaise that has befallen them all. The picture he paints is of a very human situation. But he has the strength of leadership — we might even say the charisma — to induce these early settlers to utter together this profound confession. And so they confessed how they were exhausted, depressed, deflated, and therefore quarrelsome, growling at each other (v. 11), and putting all the blame upon God for causing it all (v. 13).

Consequently, they confessed, 'justice', the practice of righteousness, 'is far from us' (v. 9). 'We look for light', for the shining of God's face, 'and behold, darkness', the darkness of evil, of *tohu*, of death. It is a case of each one for himself; and 'kindly love' (RSV 'righteousness') 'does not overtake us'. We hear only 'We . . . we . . . we': 'we grope . . . we stumble . . . we growl', even though we belong to the people whom God has 'put right' with himself. But fancy groping for God when there was no need, for God had already found them. 'Our transgressions' (acts of rebellion) keep growing in number in front of *thee*, 'our sins' (our wrong choices) keep on testifying against *us* (v. 12). We note those two opposite poles. But the 'we' here seem particularly to be those who have already defected (v. 13b), for in all this confession there is no element of that 'holier than thou' attitude which we noticed before. They are not repudiating the idea that 'it is not our responsibility that some are speaking oppression and revolt' ('defection', v. 13), or 'perverting justice' with the result that love and compassion for one's neighbour stand 'afar off', and that 'truth (mutual integrity) has fallen (literally, has been 'knocked down') in the public squares' (where the 'justices of the peace' were known to take their seat). In other words, to kick against the pricks of the Covenant is to break faith with God and his way of peace (v. 8). Thereupon evil begets evil. The one who gives himself over to 'oppression and revolt' soon finds himself in a vicious circle from which there is no escape — 'he makes himself a prey' (v. 15). Having groped and stumbled, he falls into the realm of death (v. 10). Thus his sins are no mere philosophical ideas. In fact, every one of the verbs used here describes actions, the ongoing actions of living persons, as the active participles employed here make clear. Thus a breakdown in social justice is bound to follow upon repudiation of the love of God.

Those high-minded, excited returnees, by losing faith in God's *hesed*, his steadfast love, had thereby said 'No' to the Covenant. Consequently, they had opted to call down upon themselves the curse outlined in Deuteronomy 28. Yet it was not only 'they' who had done so; 'we' too, says TI, we who make this confession have done likewise. God has made us also to be 'sin', for we all belong together in the one body (Isa. 59:15).

Modern readers would like to excise Deuteronomy 28 from the Bible. Yet here we have the historical situation that this people who have been given a second chance, named by Isaiah 'a remnant will return' (10:21-22), have now discovered by travelling the hard way: that 'salvation' is not an end state. God's people must still continue to live in the world as sinners. For, as Isaiah had said at 10:22, 'destruction is decreed' but 'overflowing'; for out of it comes *tsedaqah,* that love and care for others that brings about social 'righteousness'.

15b-19   Some individual person present at the delivery of this sermon now crowns the group confession by exclaiming that since the *hasidim,* the loyalists, also were sinners, therefore 'there was no one to intervene' in the situation. Thus he was pointing to the logical reality that only God was left to do so. He declared that at the time of the Exodus from Egypt God had found it necessary to act as the divine Warrior (Exod. 15:1-21; see Isa. 9:7; 42:13; 49:24-26; 52:10), for then God 'was appalled' (rather than RSV 'wondered').

There now follows a surprise. One expects a voice of judgment; but no. 'His own arm' alone 'brought him victory', and his own love alone is what God has relied on, what has 'upheld him'. There follows a description of the uniform of the divine Warrior (v. 17). (Paul copies this passage at Eph. 6:10-17, where he calls upon us to do what God does.) So we must look carefully to discover what exactly the 'righteousness' that God 'put on' means here. What we have is the feminine term which we examined in Isaiah 56. The reference is to God's saving love exhibited in the actions of a human being; and so also with the parallel feminine term 'salvation'. The word 'vengeance' presents the modern reader with a wrong idea. *Naqam* means 'vindication' rendered without fear or favour (cf. 35:4), for God's action is both destruction and salvation in one (cf. Luke 18:7). 'Fury' is that concentration of purpose which we call 'zeal'. Its meaning is well expressed at John 2:17 when Jesus' disciples quoted Ps. 69:9 in reference to Jesus' cleansing of the temple: 'Zeal for thy house has consumed me'.

The language of v. 18a is obscure. The RSV translates on the

basis of the Hebrew (MT). But the Versions seem to have read:
'In his own right, as LORD of all activities, he will repay (each
of) them for their actions'; that is, he will render justice to each
person as he deserves. Included here is Isaiah's awareness that
God will use as the mediator of his plan a man, a human being
(at present there was 'no man' available, v. 16), who would be
at the same time Mighty God himself (cf. Everlasting Father and
Prince of *shalom*, 9:6). That passage also concludes with the words,
'The zeal of the LORD of hosts will do this' (v. 7). Clearly such
a mediator is basic to God's plan, in that he is seen to be necessary both before and after the pattern of God's saving activity
was revealed in historical event.

Though the text of v. 19b is evidently corrupt, most commentators believe that the RSV is nearest the mark in its rendering.
God himself is the rushing wind or spirit, just as he is at Pentecost
immediately after his glory has finally been revealed (cf. John
13:31; Acts 2:2). In other words, God must complete his work of
redemption, the pattern of which has now been revealed in history even as it has been recorded and interpreted in the whole
long book of Isaiah. Yet more, now that we have seen how 'the
Isaiahs' use the word *tsedaqah*, we learn that God's power of love
which he exerts through humanity—although there was 'no man'
to help him—must yet be effective. Moreover these verses, having
been written in the 'prophetic perfect' tense, thereby show that
once God has uttered his plan the latter must necessarily work
out in space and time yet paradoxically cannot be fulfilled without a mediator.

But when his plan is finally enacted then 'the coastlands', the
gentile trading peoples around the Mediterranean, in fact all
people everywhere, 'from the rising of the sun' in the east to the
west—and so not just the covenant people—'shall fear the name
of the LORD' (the revelation of his nature as saviour) and shall
see 'his glory' (cf. 66:18; Ps. 102:15). In so declaring TI has
picked up and developed God's promise from Isa. 43:6 and 49:22.

20-21   At v. 16 we learned that God 'saw'. We learn here that
as a result 'he will come'. This then is the climax of the chapter.
TI reaches it within the progression of thought that develops
throughout the whole long book of Isaiah, which has been built
in turn upon such passages as 2 Sam. 23:2; Isa. 51:16; Ezek.

36:26-27, in full confidence of their vitality. Finally, he develops this climactic scene to new heights in Isaiah 63.

In one breath we are told that God will come 'like a rushing stream' and then that 'he will come to Zion as Redeemer', that is, he will sweep in in his capacity as Redeemer. He will come 'to those in Jacob', a careful choice of words. For it is to Jacob, and not to Israel, that he will come. The whole bent of Jacob's nature had been to rebel (*pasha'*; RSV *'transgression'* is used wrongly here); *pasha'* describes the human action of breaking the Covenant that God had made with his people. But at a particular historical occasion God had wrestled all night with Jacob in a desert place (Gen. 32:24-30). As a human creature made in God's own image Jacob had inherited God's freedom of will. In the bout God had freely allowed Jacob to win. Yet God used that moment to reveal that his grace was greater than Jacob's victory, and so God forgave the egotistical sinner. Being a forgiven man Jacob now needed a new name to describe his new condition (v. 28). At Isa. 59:20 then the Redeemer 'will' now 'come' to the forgiven and renewed community, the New Israel that bears Jacob's name. Moreover, what we read of here is an absolute and unconditional promise of God (*neum Yahweh*); or, as Luke 1:73 interprets it, it is God's 'oath', in that his promise is clothed in the framework of his eternal Covenant. Let us note the following:

(a) Some scholars suggest that Isaiah of Jerusalem was not interested in the Mosaic covenant, in that he never once refers to it. The word occurs only at 24:5, a verse which is not from Isaiah's pen; his phrase at 28:15, 18, a 'covenant with death', uses the word with a different connotation. However, his utterances are full of terms that can be understood only in a covenantal context.

(b) DI, on the other hand, makes God himself refer to the Covenant at 42:6; 49:8; 54:10; 55:3.

(c) Now we note that TI makes four references to it, at 56:4, 6; 61:8, and here at 59:21. Here it takes its natural place in the utterances of a prophet who, preaching about the years 536-525 B.C., is now bringing to a head the whole theology of the Isaian school that had developed and been enunciated ever since 740. For TI, however, the Covenant is a mere instrument. No one loves it, rejoices in it, philosophizes about it. It is the Giver of the Covenant whom one loves and rejoices in because of his *emet*, his faithfulness to his Covenant. This, then, is why it must last forever and cannot be thought to be of only temporary value, and why there can be only one Covenant that will never be revoked. For God never changes (Mal. 3:6).

Israel, of course, already possesses two gifts from God, 'my spirit which is upon you' and 'my words which I have put in your mouth', and these shall belong to you and to your children's children 'from this time forth and for evermore'. Yet God's Word and God's Spirit are 'in' and 'upon you' only because they have been channelled there through the Covenant. The logic is, therefore, that God's Covenant is like the exoskeleton of a lobster, which may have to be shed more than once in the lobster's life; but the animal itself within remains constant. Jeremiah had looked for a new 'exoskeleton' to take the place of the Mosaic covenant of old (Jer. 31:33). In a parallel manner Paul speaks of 'the new man' in Christ as *kainos*, the man with the new exoskeleton (e.g., Eph. 2:15). He does not use the word *neos* ('new, fresh'), for that adjective would imply that once Jacob had wrestled with God he had become a different being. But *kainos* preserves the idea that the forgiven man, though still the same old flesh-and-blood Jacob, is instead related to God in a new way, the way of forgiveness.

The Covenant, as TI experienced and understood it, was to be completely comprehensive, even as Ezekiel had declared a generation earlier (Ezek. 34:25, where the word *shalom* is used to represent its root meaning of 'whole' or 'complete'). Thus it would include within its scope all nations, as well as both matter and spirit, heaven and earth (see Isa. 65:17), both life now and life in eternity.

This mighty reality, TI says, is to be explained by parents to children in endless succession down through the years, thus making it ever clearer that it is the family unit with which God has chosen to deal, in that it is only out of such that the 'chosen' individual can emerge. So it is a mark here of saving grace that our speaker consistently uses the word 'we'. As the philosopher Friedrich Schelling put it nearly two centuries ago, 'Individuality is sin'; or, better, TI introduces us to understand Jesus' prayer, 'Our Father who art in heaven'.

The 'movement' of the Covenant, from now on therefore, took a new direction within the New Israel. What had now happened was the fulfilment of Moses' longing cry (Num. 11:29): 'Would that all the LORD'S people were prophets, that the LORD would put his spirit upon them'. TI comments in consequence: 'My spirit . . . shall not depart out of your mouth, or . . . of your children'. Thus we have come to the end of the line, historically speaking, of the great individual prophets. From now on the office of the interpreter of the Word was to be shared by the ordinary family both as part of their life on earth as well as in the life to come.

The Return and the reestablishment of Jerusalem ought to have been a cosmic event. As it turned out, it was only a shabby affair, to use Yehezkel Kaufmann's choice of words. Yet it was TI's faith, as Kaufmann goes on to declare, that it was also a 'crypto-cosmic' event. For the ultimate significance of the event God, in his good time, would reveal through his unshakable loyalty to his Covenant, and it would be interpreted down the ages through the lips of little children within the 'covenantal' fellowship of the happy home.

CHAPTER 60

THE FIRST LIGHT OF THE NEW DAWN
Isaiah 60:1-22

1-3 'Arise, shine; for thy light has come'; we use the singular 'thy' to remind us that the Hebrew uses that form. God is addressing 'those in Jacob who turn from transgression' (59:20) as one people of God.

Throughout the OT light and salvation are synonymous, light being the sacramental sign of God's redemptive love. TI is here addressing — with these words! — his dispirited and rebellious fellow citizens gathered in a cleared space amongst the ruins. Taking his text, we might suppose, from his predecessor's great material, he raises his voice above all the natural noises that inhibit preaching in the open air and repeats the now well-loved words: 'I have given you (not as RSV) as a covenant to the people (of the earth), a light to the nations' (49:6, 8). 'So now', he says, 'Arise (*qumi*), my daughter Zion' (the verb is in the feminine singular; cf. Mark 5:41) from the 'death' of the Exile. You are now saved (43:1); you have been raised from the grave (Ezek. 37:13). You may regard the ruins around you as the grave of a city, yet do believe that 'the glory of the LORD has risen upon you (Isa. 60:2 author's translation)', the glory that had departed when Jerusalem fell (Ezek. 3:12-13, 22-23), but which Ezekiel had declared would return when God would once again dwell there (48:35). 'Darkness keeps on covering (not 'shall cover' RSV) the earth, and thick darkness (*'araphel*, the blackness of chaos) the peoples' (with reference to Exod. 10:21-23; cf. John 1:5); 'but the LORD is now spreading out his rays of light upon thee, and his glory will be visible over thee' (author's translation; cf. Isa. 9:2). And so TI continues in this vein with constant quotations from chs. 40– 55.

God's 'glory' is described like the haze of dazzling light which partially hides, partially reveals the rising sun, that 'will be seen *resting* upon you'. It is because of that, that the nations will come to 'you' (always feminine singular), not because of anything of value in 'you' yourself. In other words, TI is now enlarging upon the wonder of God's *tsedeq* that he first discussed in ch. 56.

All this means then that the 'glory' has now in fact returned, and is now actually arising 'upon you' like the rays of the morning sun at the dawn of a new day. Once again, God has acted first — 'your light has come'. Consequently Israel is now 'to do unto others what God has done to them'. Israel must now, in their turn, 'shine' like a lighthouse to lighten the path of all nations as they 'come to your light' (cf. Rev. 21:11, 24) and kings as they see 'the brightness of your (!) rising'. We recall the words of Jesus at Matt. 5:14-16: 'You are the light of the world. . . . Let your light so shine . . .'.

Again, the sincere scepticism that some Jews feel about the Christian understanding of God's action in Christ can be allayed by this passage. The problem is that the NT claims that 'the Messiah has come'. On the other hand, it can be said that the world has certainly not been redeemed in that people have not become any less wicked. Isaian theology, however, has presented us with the revelation in history of God's ultimate pattern of his redemptive purpose and activity for the salvation of mankind. That pattern had now reached its completion in TI's day. So we would expect, if we hold this Jewish view of the ways of God, that the world would have been 'saved' by the year 538 B.C. Yet Isaiah 57 shows how not only Israel but the gentile peoples too were still just as wicked as ever, even though God's recreative act of love was now revealed. What this Jewish view of the messianic act of Christ thus fails to recognize is that while God's *tsedeq* ('putting right') is made complete in the death and resurrection of Christ, God requires the return commitment of his elect people within the Covenant to live out his *tsedaqah* ('creative love'). They are to do so in the power of his Spirit and by faith alone, if the completion of God's 'plan' is to be reached: 'by faith alone', for we who believe — Jew and Christian alike — are meant to live out the calling we have received at 58:6-9, despite the continuance of the darkness. For only 'then shall your light break forth' (v. 8).

The Road Home to God (4-7)

Our preacher invites his congregation, standing there amongst the ruins, to use their sanctified imagination and see, not the ruins, but *people*, 'radiant' with joy at seeing what God's love has performed — fathers, mothers, teenagers and little babies together streaming home to Zion. Does this picture refer merely to returning Israel, or does it extend to Israel's former enemies as well? Do these verses emphasise the particularism of TI's meanings, or do they also include his universalism? It may well be that here he is holding the two emphases together in tension.

The phrase 'carried in the arms' (v. 4) means really 'nursed on the hip'. At its root the verb 'carried' actually has the idea of being faithful, reliable and true. Connecting it with what precedes, we envisage Mother Zion stretching out her arms like the rays of the early morning sun to receive all these babies in love, even as God has now received her. Zion's action would then reveal the *shalom* which God had promised would follow upon his act of redemption (57:19), and which would also reveal the perfect union of mankind with their environment (cf. Hos. 2:18; Ezek. 34:25). Zion's economic life too would thus know God's *shalom* as the nations contributed their quota to it. 'Midian' means just 'Arabs', multitudes of whom would come with their camels bringing their 'wealth' as their token of love. Those coming by 'sea' included the legendary 'Sheba' (Ps. 72:10-15 shows why they would want to come). 'Nebaioth' was the home of the Ishmaelites, Israel's hereditary enemies. They too would come with gifts of 'rams' to lay upon 'my altar'.

Now we point to the reason why we have consistently employed the feminine singular 'thou', as it is in the Hebrew. For it is to the bride of Yahweh that the nations will bring their wealth, the bride in whom God has hidden himself in self-emptying love (45:14-15) and to whom he has now revealed his glory (as at John 13:31) by emptying himself out as an *asham*, a sin-offering for 'many' (Isa. 53:10). The nations that 'come up to you' do so not to honour Israel but to 'proclaim', or 'herald', the praise of Yahweh (v. 6d; cf. Matt. 2:10-11 and Luke 2:20) for having revealed his saving love (cf. Isa. 49:18). The meaning of this passage has often been deliberately misrepresented as the self-glorification of the Jewish people. On the other hand, it is only after having 'come in out of the cold' or, rather, having been brought in by members of the New Israel that the outsider can discover the joy of faith and obedience. In his reply to the Canaanite woman at Matt. 15:21-28 Jesus made this reality explicit.

We go on to read that God receives the offerings of the nations 'with acceptance'. This phrase means 'in accordance with my plan', which was that enunciated by DI in days before: 'To me every knee shall bow, every tongue shall swear' (Isa. 45:23). Yet, since this passage is eschatological in purpose, more must be said. The People of God were to be a kingdom of priests (Exod. 19:6), not just to the nations but actually to all creation, as Teilhard de Chardin delights to point out; for these 'who love him', as Paul believes, are the ones 'who are called according to his purpose' or 'plan' (Rom. 8:28). When that happens, then 'I (God, not Israel) will *be glorified in* my glorious house' (author's translation).

8-14 The Mediterranean Sea is pictured as dotted with the white sails of ships bringing home '*thy* sons from afar', the large trading vessels known as 'ships of Tarshish' leading the way. The Mediterranean isles too—inhabited by Gentiles—have been eagerly waiting for this opportunity to come to me (says God); they are saying, 'Please, we want to help in the building of Zion' or, as we might say today, 'in the building of the kingdom of God' (see 51:5; 55:5). Their gifts, both those of Israelites and of Gentiles, are the freewill offerings of human beings who are thrilled that God has revealed his 'name'—his character, his nature—by redeeming and thus glorifying Israel. This is of course the order of redemption throughout the Bible, as we see at Matt. 10:1; Rom. 1:16; Rev. 2:25-26. For the RSV rendering 'with their kings led in procession' (Isa. 60:11d) we might read, with John Skinner and others, 'with their kings leading the way'. Historically, this is how much of Europe was evangelized. For example, St. Columba first converted the pagan king of northern Scotland, whereupon his people followed their king's example. On the other hand, some commentators suggest that vv. 10-12 speak of the judgment of God upon those Gentiles who would not 'minister to you' (v. 10) or 'serve you' (v. 12).

At 45:14 DI had envisaged that the riches of the Gentiles 'shall come over to you (Zion, feminine singular) and be yours, they shall follow you; they shall come over in chains and bow down to you'. Some expositors assume that Israel would capture these foreigners in war and take booty from them. This, however, is not likely, in light of the context of the passage. (1) The foreigners 'shall come over', not 'shall be brought over', evidently unwillingly. They shall gladly follow you, it seems. (2) 'They will make supplication to you' — the Servant of the LORD, and the Bride of the LORD — saying 'God is *in* you only (not 'with' you, as RSV). (3) The Gentiles are 'captivated' by God's love or, as the French would say, *enchaine*, 'chained', 'linked' to Israel by it. (4) They declare in awe what Israel themselves had never recognized: 'Truly the divine Being (*el*) is *in* you, and in no other'. Then they continue, 'Truly thou, the divine Being, hidest thyself as the God and Savior of Israel'. The Gentiles have come to worship this strange God, who has hidden himself within the loving bonds of the Covenant he had long concluded with his people Israel, and with them alone. In light of this understanding of DI's words, 60:8-14 is to be read theologically and not politically.

'Your gates shall be open continually', so that no matter when the tired pilgrims should arrive they may be welcomed 'home'. 'Gates' implies walls rebuilt. It was foreigners who had destroyed Jerusalem's walls, so it was only justice that foreigners should rebuild them. An eye for an eye is an expression of justice that we dare not suppose we can outgrow. What we must do is see how God transfers the penalty to another (ch. 53) but does not ignore the evil done as if it were of no account. He may even use the evil done to recreate the situation anew, as here! For the words 'in my favor' (60:10) mean 'as part of my plan'. As a corollary, those who refuse to 'build up your walls' must necessarily suffer the judgment that has been expressed so firmly in the Torah. Imagine refusing to join the reconstruction of that one spot on earth which was now called 'the place of God's feet' (v. 13); for it was there *and there only* that the ultimate revelation of the divine mind was to be given to a stricken world (cf. Luke 18:31; John 1:14) — a revelation, as TI has noted before, that would affect even the trees in mankind's environment.

Solomon was the first to employ the beautiful cedars of Lebanon, 'the glory of Lebanon' (v. 13), to adorn the sanctuary of Yahweh. His action was thus a pointer to the future. 'The pine' here is the tall, handsome Cilician fir, a beautiful tree. And so

Zion will be a 'glorious' reality, the centrepoint of meaning for all creation; and as such it will be known, not by its political title of Jerusalem, but by its theological designation, 'The City of the LORD, The Zion of the Holy One of Israel'.

The Mighty One of Jacob (15-18)

Our prophet had before this built up his picture out of earlier declarations (e.g. 1:21; 49:14, 21; 54:6, 11) of a city seemingly 'forsaken and hated', with no one interested enough even to visit its ruins. Now however he declares on God's behalf, 'I will make thee (feminine) "exaltation", "magnificence" '. The latter word (*geon*) seeks to express what is beyond human imagination. To it, moreover, is added the word *'olam*, which connotes more than 'forever' — if the human mind imagines that meaning only to indicate endless time — for it is an eschatological term and speaks of what is beyond space and time. Beginning as a material city, Jerusalem will be supplied by products produced by all other material and historical cities; but only because Jerusalem is in reality 'The City of the Saviour' of all mankind. Yahweh is not only now becoming Zion's Saviour; he has always been such. He is the Redeemer of Jacob, who lived a thousand years before TI's day (cf. John 8:58). And he will be the Redeemer 'from age to age', because — as we shall see at Isaiah 63 — his right arm, thrust into space and time (a very useful picture for our limited human minds) may appear at any juncture in history coming forth from the eternal 'now'.

Now follows a 'theological' reversal of roles: 'Instead of. . . .' The despair and pessimism expressed in such a passage as Lam. 2:15 by a man who had lived through the destruction of the city is here, not just reversed, but is used as a springboard to present us with what is positively new — with the revelation of the nature of the Redeemer, the Mighty One of Jacob. The 'instead-ofs' move forward from space-time and material substances into aspects of ultimate eschatological significance. 'I will make your overseers *shalom*' (Israel's state of peace once they have learned how to live by showing *tsedaqah*, loving concern for others now that they have experienced God's *tsedeq*, his redemptive love for them). With memories of what 'taskmasters' were like in the days of Moses in Egypt, the reality of the springboard becomes clear. Those insolent and cruel sadists are to become *tsedaqah* itself! Can we imagine this applying to the guards at Auschwitz? Since 'violence' and 'destruction' are now things of the past, stone walls are not needed for defence. Saving creative love of neighbour (*yeshu'ah*, the feminine term) takes their place; for if one loves his or her enemy there will be no need to defend oneself from him. Nor will Israel now need city gates, for people will enter the Holy City just by praising the God of Israel.

19-22a Building upon ch. 35 and upon Isaiah's ability to show how God creates out of negation (1:18; cf. 49:19-21; 54:11) and how he can use the reversal of roles (49:23, 26), TI offers further illustrations to develop from Isaiah's faith this theme that 'a remnant will return' (10:21). We note that he employs abstract nouns such as 'peace', 'righteousness', 'praise' and makes scientifically impossible predictions (v. 19). Thus we are aware that it is a poet who is speaking, not literally but metaphorically, even — dare we suggest — sacramentally, about the grace of a God whose loving purpose can never be adequately described in human terms.

Verse 21 brings into the picture the ultimate outcome of the Covenant. 'Thy (feminine) people shall all be *tsaddiqim*', all having been 'put right' by God's acts of *tsedeq* for which he created the Covenant. (We note how Revelation 21 pictures the ultimate outcome of this passage.) But the promises of God extended, within the Covenant, to 'the land' as well. It too is to have eschatological significance. Mankind cannot be separated from the environment. Their nature and character are always influenced by geographical, climatic, and social conditions. Isaiah's parable of the vineyard (5:1-7) does not distinguish between Israel as vine and Israel as vineyard. Nowhere in the OT is it supposed that persons are mere naked souls who can be saved apart from their 'land' or environment. Ps. 80:14-15 speaks of Israel as God's 'planting', the vine that he had brought up from Egypt. Thus Israel's roots are now in 'the land'. Israel is a *'shoot' (netser)* that grows up out of the soil (cf. Isa. 53:2). A pun upon this word occurs at 49:6, where *natsir* is translated 'preserved'. Israel had been preserved in the land, the soil, of Babylon, awaiting the redemption and restoration that had now occurred. In fact, God had needed and had actually used the soil, the environment, of Babylon to create his new action of restoration. And he had done so from the beginning, for ever since 'the least' and 'the smallest' — Abraham — had claimed 'the land' under God (Gen. 12:7),

God had included it in his plan and purpose to use Israel for the redemption of the world.

Contemporary with TI there appeared in India the figure of Vardhamana Jnatriputra Mahavira. With a band of twenty-three followers this man broke from Hinduism to found the Jain religion. Amongst much else, Jainism taught the transmigration of the soul, a doctrine to be found of course amongst many other peoples both then and now. Such a doctrine was possible provided a person's soul was regarded as existing in its own right, whether there be a God or not. Isaian theology, by contrast, declares two opposite realities about the human person. First, being a sinner, one is a 'disintegrated personality' who can fall into 'nonbeing' (6:5 KJV 'undone'; see commentary at 59:1-8). Second, since a person is God's creature, he or she is therefore the object of God's love. Yet that person is not a 'mere' soul but rather what we would call 'a person in his or her environment', and it is as such that the person remains the object of God's love for all eternity. No wonder the Eastern religions as a whole are unable to grasp the biblical doctrine of the resurrection of the body. At this point, therefore, by giving all the glory to God alone, TI has set in motion a concept of God's recreative love for his human creatures such as empowers them to be remade from 'lost' objects into new people for his own glory!

Yahweh's Signature (22b)

All the above is to take place for one end only, 'that I might be glorified' (v. 21b). As we have learned before, it is to take place 'in' Israel! For God has humbled himself, has emptied himself to remain hidden in the people of his choice. So this majestic poem concludes by the addition of Yahweh's signature, so to speak, and by his promise to bring its contents to pass quickly, suddenly (RSV 'hasten'), at the appropriate time. Yet what does that mean? What does 'in its time' signify?

The last couplet of ch. 60, expressed in terms of a promise, enframes the whole chapter by underlining the great announcement made at v. 1, even as it shows that the cosmic-redemptive language of vv. 1-3 is no exaggeration. Yet God's signature is applied to a revelation that can be accepted only if Israel really believes that God knows what he is doing as he makes his plans for the future of his world (cf. Mark 13:32).

CHAPTER 61

THE GOOD NEWS
Isaiah 61:1-11

Chapter 61 expands the contents of the preceding chapter by picking up key words found within it. Thus it flows straight on from ch. 60. Also it seems to take for granted that the congregation addressed would be acquainted with DI's message at 42:1-4 and 49:1-6.

The Spirit of God (1-4)

There is no need to ask who is speaking here, for the language of this unit has already been used to describe the calling of God's Servant people, Israel. 'Me' is both TI and Israel at once. DI's earlier interpretation of that task is underlined now in TI's very first statement: 'The Spirit of the Lord GOD (or 'Yahweh' in the Hebrew) is upon me' (cf. 11:2; 42:1). The Spirit comes, not descending like the gentle dew, but 'pushing', 'impelling', as we see for example at Judg. 13:25.

Theologians have dubbed the Spirit in the OT 'God's tempest'. Nowhere is it shown to be an intellectual or mental power, nor is it a higher principle controlling human nature. Gen. 1:2 is translated by some scholars: 'A stormy wind raged over the waters', a raging storm keeping the waters of chaos in flux and preventing them from emerging in any defined shape or form. As Isa. 30:28 puts it, the Spirit is like an 'overflowing stream', just as it is pictured also in the famous promise of the outpouring of the Spirit 'on all flesh' at Joel 2:28-29. In the OT the Spirit always overpowers a person 'from outside'. It then leaves him again. Thus the OT has a 'dynamistic' view of the Spirit. Modern people would even say that in the OT the Spirit is not just 'psychic' but a thoroughly physical force. TI's hearers would almost feel the Spirit like oil on their heads (cf. Psalm 133). So

50

we see from this and from kindred passages that the Hebrew mind, in this case the Isaian tradition, is more interested in acting than in being, in the dynamic than in the static, in the historical than in the speculative, in the revelatory than in the world of ideas. Consequently all that the Servant people are anointed here to say and to do they perform not on their own initiative nor in their own strength. All that happens to them or through them is of grace, of the power of grace, in a manner that no humanist need try to claim mankind can do of themselves. In fact, mankind's great sin is in resisting the awesome might of the Spirit and in not having the faith and the loyalty to let the Spirit act through them. Clearly this is why Jesus has to say that this offer of God had only then been fulfilled — filled full — in himself, for in him alone do we find the total obedience to the Spirit that we read of in Luke 4:21. (We note that this Lucan passage is prefaced by the words: 'And Jesus returned in the *power* of the Spirit' [v. 14].)

God himself then purposes to act in and through Israel his instrument so that his plan for humankind may bring about *shalom* in human society. He can produce it actually out of the misery, greed, and violence that rule human life, and out of 'man's inhumanity to man'. God can do this, it seems, only by entering into the human scene himself. He does not intend to utter a fiat from the sky, while himself remaining outside of the misery of humanity. Again, by opening TI's eyes to the significance of the ruins of Jersualem, God had taught him to think in sacramental terms. To rebuild the old waste places (6:11; 61:4) was but one side of the coin; the other was the rebuilding of mankind as a whole. God had set Israel free, our poet now grasps clearly, in order that in the power of the Spirit Israel might set all other peoples free. For this is what being anointed is basically for. God had anointed Cyrus (45:1), giving him the power to set Israel free; now it was Israel's turn.

Israel's task is manifold, but all aspects of it rest upon their having been anointed to act. Prophets were anointed to be prophets, not to sit still and enjoy fellowship with God.

(a) Israel has been commissioned 'to bring good tidings to the afflicted'. The fact that the RSV mg reads 'poor' for 'afflicted' shows that this word (*'anawim*) too is like a double-headed coin, and it explains how it can be rendered by two different Greek

51

expressions at Matt. 5:3, 5 and Luke 6:20. At Isa. 66:2 again this
word is rendered by 'humble', only to be interpreted at once by
'contrite in spirit', meaning those whose basic egotism has been
drained out of them (cf. Ps. 37:11). The good news is not a
summons to people to believe in God. Such a call is not good
news at all; it can only exasperate the hearer. Rather, Israel is
to tell the world what God the Saviour has already done for them
as a first step in his loving plan for all humankind. But basic to
all that Israel is to say is that which follows from ch. 40, where
we learn that God has first acted to forgive sinners who are alien-
ated from himself, and to bring them home.

(b) 'He has sent me.' This is how God always works (e.g.,
Exod. 3:10; John 3:17; cf. Isa. 50:4). He 'sends out', extends his
'self' into human flesh, thereby employing that flesh by moti-
vating it to do his will.

(c) The instruction 'to bind up the brokenhearted' provides
a picture of what God is like in himself (cf. Ps. 147:3). Israel's
ministry is thus to be a ministry of grace. Both Judaism and
Christianity are aware that to forgive sins is to heal. We possess
the great declaration of the rabbinical tradition: 'No man can
recover from illness till his sins are remitted'. Thus even when
the ruined city confronted our poet with a tremendous challenge,
God enabled him to see that the central issue was one of forgiveness and of a renewed life.

(d) 'To proclaim liberty to the captives' had been the great
message of DI (cf. also 58:6). Yet it was only based on the words
of Torah (Lev. 25:8-55) and then applied to the release of Israel
when they were held captive in Babylon. But by now, by his act
of *tsedeq*, God had set captive Israel free. As God's Servant, therefore, Israel was now, in the spirit of *tsedaqah*, to set free the rest
of mankind. We should note that Jesus made use of this verse to
demonstrate that the kingdom had come with himself, though he
used not the word 'Spirit' but 'finger of God' to show God's
intervention in history (Luke 11:20).

(e) Israel is also to proclaim 'the opening of the prison'. The
RSV mg guides the reader to recognize a difficulty here with the
text. What we have is 'and to the prisoners "very much opening" '
or 'smashing open'. This is a usage that employs a peculiar
reduplicated form of the verb. At Isa. 42:7 and 49:9 opening the
doors of a prison and opening the eyes of the blind are clearly

regarded as one, in that a prisoner in those days was held captive in the terrible darkness of a dungeon. The nations are thus regarded here as all being prisoners held in darkness until the light of God shines on them through the cooperation of Zion (60:1-2). This task laid upon Israel is thus to be an intense one of hard work for God, and work which is *of* God. Through his Spirit God has now invited his elect people to enter into the fellowship of loving active participation in the service of the needy that he himself knows and which he expressed so long before to Moses: 'But I will be with you' (Exod. 3:12).

(f) Israel's service is 'to those who are bound'. Because of the 'sacramental' thinking of the author we see that he was speaking both of prisoners physically detained and of people bound as slaves to their own egotism, lusts, and mutual antagonisms. The modern Western reader finds it difficult to break from the heritage of thought received in his or her state school education, in those lands where the biblical revelation is excluded from the curriculum. It is this Greek heritage that the secularist takes for granted as being at the basis of Western civilization. The Greeks, if one may speak generally, divided reality in two. They separated between the ideal world and the world of things, between heaven and earth, between 'this world' and 'the next world', between matter and spirit, body and soul, the realm of science and the realm of theology, and so on. That kind of thinking was not the world of the 'Isaiahs', for to them creation was one unity. So when the modern reader asks: 'Did the speaker refer to those bound in the darkness of a prison cell, or to those bound by the cords of selfishness in spiritual darkness?' he raises a question that does not belong in the OT. The salvation of the 'soul' (a word for which Hebrew has no equivalent) or even such ideas as one finds in the East of the immortality of the soul or the transmigration of the soul are concepts rooted in pagan and not in biblical thought or revelation.

(g) 'To proclaim the year of the LORD'S favour' is to be understood in connection with the setting free of slaves (Lev. 25:10). It seems that in the Near East generally an amnesty was proclaimed when prisoners were released at the inauguration of a new king's reign. When Evil-merodach king of Babylon thus showed favour (*ratson*) to Jehoiachin, the last king of Judah, the editor of 2 Kings regarded his act as first glimpse of dawn for the exiles in the darkness of their foreign captivity (2 Kgs. 25:27). This Babylonian king even 'killed for him the fatted calf'. Interestingly, the word 'liberty' (*deror*) at Isa. 61:1 can also mean 'swallow' (the variety of bird), as if (in our English idiom) this first swallow, this first act of renewal, were a sign of a new spring to come.

At Lev. 25:10 we read: 'And you shall hallow the fiftieth year, and proclaim liberty throughout the land to all its inhabitants; it shall be a jubilee for you, when each of you shall return to his property and . . . to his family'. Cyrus' decree had marked just such a jubilee. It had now been proclaimed exactly fifty years after the fall of Jerusalem. The people had been released and restored to their families and to their property. The original year of jubilee had been intended as a sign of the *eschaton*, of the sabbath of God's eternal rest (Gen. 2:2). Now this newly occurred historical event was to be the sign of God's 'year of favour' for all mankind. The good news which the New Israel was to proclaim was thus certainly not to be understood in terms of 'religion' or of a promise of a world hereafter. It was to be understood as an event that would arise from this historical fact, and was to continue to be effective within Israel's historical experience. This, of course, is what Jesus meant when he declared, in quoting this passage about himself, 'Today this scripture has been fulfilled in your hearing' (Luke 4:21).

But what we are to hold onto at the moment is that Israel has been anointed within the covenant relationship to be a covenant to the people (Isa. 49:6) *now*. Israel's task is not to be carried forward in a spirit of triumphalism (as some commentators seem to think). Israel's task is to teach, preach, and serve from TI's day onwards. Unlike modern people, who suppose that 'the gospel' is concerned with religion and ethics, TI's gospel is concerned with revelation, obedience, and love. One aspect of *tsedaqah*, the word used to describe the human action resulting from God's act (*tsedeq*) examined in ch. 56, is well described in the rabbinical saying at *Aboth* ii.21: 'It is not up to you to complete the work, but neither are you free to desist from it'. In other words, as the rabbis declared, the yoke of the Covenant reveals a prevenient grace that demands Israel's total obedience.

But total obedience to what? We note that there is no divine command here to keep the commandments, or to use outward signs or symbols such as circumcision or the sacrifice of bulls.

This is because the Covenant itself is the one and only sign of God's purpose of love that we need (cf. Ezek. 34:25-31). Thus since the Covenant is ordained to embrace all mankind (47:21-23), TI believes that the 'covenant with death' of which Isaiah spoke (Isa. 28:14-22) has now been annulled by God's action through Cyrus. As God's 'messiah', his 'anointed' (45:1), Cyrus had been instrumental in laying in Zion a new foundation, a precious cornerstone: 'He who believes will not be in haste'. Thus Israel had been set free only by 'God's strange work' (28:21) in identifying himself with his Servant Israel when the latter was in 'prison' in Babylon.

But there was a reason for Israel's being set free. Any 'theology of liberation' must take that reason into account. God had a purpose and plan from the foundation of the world (51:16) to use his people in his passionate concern for all his human creatures. Thus in ch. 61 we are made to see that TI has 'brought forth' (Jesus' term at Matt. 13:23) a new *torah* out of the old. He has already demonstrated in Isaiah 57 how the human situation is such that laws to control society are necessary, in fact that 'law' must come before 'gospel'. But his new *torah* accepts that the 'law of Moses' is fulfilled in the one law that subsumes all others — the law of love (Deut. 6:4-5; Mark 12:29-31). TI believes he has discovered this to be so, not by his own reasoning, but by the Spirit of the LORD (Isa. 61:1). This means that, by revelation, he sees that ethics is not an absolute in itself. Ethical action cannot be classified or controlled by any religious or philosophical system, for it is the fruit of love (*tsedaqah*) applied to every possible human situation. It is also performed, as God wills it to be by those who have experienced his *tsedeq*, through the power of the Spirit that has come upon them.

It was this essential significance of the new foundation that the Zadokites, those priests who traced back their authority to Aaron, could not grasp (E. Achtemeier, *The Community and Message of Isaiah 56 – 66*). They were clearly amongst those who now opposed TI as he preached the gospel of 'liberty to the captives'. Yet all these 'acts of God' had needed a *melits*, as DI had called himself at 43:27, an 'interpreter' (Gen. 42:23), an intermediary between God and mankind (Job 33:23), an ambassador (2 Chr. 32:31). Now, says TI, the LORD has anointed 'me' to do just this for the New Israel so that the People of God might perform the same task of interpreting God's purpose of love to the world. To this end, therefore, TI uses history as his textbook.

(h) Furthermore, Israel is to herald 'the day of vengeance of our God', the day of vindication, of rescue, when God will faithfully bring forth justice (42:3c; 63:4; cf. 34:8; 35:4). This 'day' had begun when the prophet first brought God's comfort to Israel, now that his act of *tsedeq* was complete (40:1).

(i) The Servant people are 'to comfort all who mourn'. Here again is a case not just of talking but of doing, of giving oneself to others, an act that can of course be a costly thing. Comfort is one aspect of the principle of justice, described as it is in the 'good-brought-forth-out-of-evil' pictures of reality noted before as well as here (61:3-4). In these descriptions we see the principle we have noted stemming from 1:18: (1) *'a garland instead of ashes'* or, as George Herbert Box translated it many years ago, 'a coronal instead of a coronach', meaning to allow the Word to be placed like a garland on the head of those living in the doldrums of life. (2) *'the mantle of praise'*, the wedding garment of joy. Placing the two phrases together, we get a picture of the custom in OT times of putting ashes on one's head when in sorrow or mourning, to be replaced by a tiara and a wedding garment. (3) *'oaks of righteousness (tsedeq)'*, great strong trees, deeply rooted in God's saving love. Such was the reality in faith of the constitution of the New Israel (cf. 60:21). The biblical oak was an evergreen tree that never shed its leaves, unlike the European oak; it always seemed to remain 'alive'. In all these cases, we should note, what we have is a renewal of the old, not of something wholly different, the same pattern as is seen in the relation between the 'New' Testament (*kaine diatheke*), understood in this sense, and the Old. Thus, having now been 'born again' by the divine act of *tsedeq*, God's people Israel now need, and actually receive, the new name of 'oaks'. Moreover, it was the LORD who planted them, not for their sakes but for his own sake, that his name might be glorified amongst the nations of the earth.

4 As noted above, the thinking in a verse like this is quite other than that of the gentile world. The rebuilding of Jerusalem (cf. 49:8) out of the present ruins represents both the literal building up again of the ancient buildings and the spiritual renewal of the people who live in the city.

Moreover, we see that God leaves humans to do the building; 'God may feed the sparrows, but he does not throw their food into the nest'. Mankind has to work as well as pray for the fulfilment of the phrase 'Thy kingdom come . . . on earth'. But they can do so only in the power of the Spirit (61:1), on the ground that they are created in the likeness of the Creator (Gen. 1:27). Thus mankind's recreative work ('build up', 'raise up', 'repair') under God's blessing becomes a sign of the eschatological future, which is always that of bringing forth new things out of the old (cf. Matt. 13:52).

In all this, moreover, we should note that TI never talks either of mankind or of 'society' in the abstract. TI is concerned with the concrete, with poor, unhappy, disillusioned, hungry *persons*, no two of whom are alike. It is these, not 'society', whom God desires to adopt as his children.

The Second Aspect of God's Comfort (5-7)

Having illuminated God's efforts to vindicate Israel and renew them, now TI turns his searchlight on the gentile peoples. There is no suggestion here of the damnation of unbelievers or such like. The Return from exile had been the sign of God's forgiving, renewing love for Israel *in the first place*. But it cannot stop at that point; it must extend to all people. God's special relationship with Israel is one of function, not of favouritism. As an element in the Covenant, Israel is to be 'a kingdom of priests' (Exod. 19:6) — priests both to God and to mankind. Israel is to do priestly service to the nations by living out before their eyes the *tsedeq*, the saving love of God. The task of the preexilic priest had been to teach each new generation of Israelites the terms of the Covenant (Deut. 33:10). Now it was the task of the New Israel, as a kingdom of priests, to let the whole world know about the love of God, and to do so by their own *tsedaqah* towards all foreigners (Isaiah 56). And Israel was to do so in such a manner that people 'shall speak of you' in recognition of this ministerial task.

We pause once again to recognize what a unique emphasis came into the world in TI's period. It is one that his contemporaries in the field of religious innovation knew nothing of, whether in India, Persia, or China. A Chinese professor, Woon Swee Tin, has recently described the Confucian code of ethics that was born about the year 550 B.C.: 'It is a closed system that puts excessive emphasis on filial piety, chastity, material achievement, loyalty to family and moderation to the point of insensitivity'. In contrast, Vatican Council II acknowledges as the continuing outcome of God's command in this chapter of Isaiah 'the emergence here of a new humanism, one in which man is defined first of all in terms of his responsibility towards his brothers and toward history' (*Gaudium et spes*, no. 55).

So we note that it is Israel who is to do the building of the kingdom of God on earth, that the Gentiles are only to supply the nuts and bolts — and all for the sake of the poor of the world. Isaiah 66:21 goes somewhat further and hopes that Gentiles will actually share with Israel in the building of Zion.

Aliens then were to attend to the physical needs of Israel while the Servant people did the building, by offering the 'wealth of the nations' in God's service. It is this phrase that supplied Adam Smith some two hundred years ago with the title of his famous study on economics. As a Christian he had come to realize for what ends God had created the wealth of the nations at all. So here, 'the laborer deserves his wages' (Luke 10:7). Yet Israel must play fair with the Gentiles and be a worthy and faithful priest to the nations. Since priest and minister are equated here, TI infers that Israel is to show all humankind what it means to 'go up to the mountain of the LORD' and to 'walk in his paths' (Isa. 2:3).

TI then rounds off his sermon by reporting God's promise to give his people a 'double portion' of good in place of 'double for all her sins', the words with which DI had begun his thesis (40:2).

God's Justice (8-9)

Now we see how God's total forgiveness reveals what God means by justice. We learn that justice can be understood only as an aspect of love: 'I the LORD love justice'. It is further explained in terms of God's hate: 'I hate "the rape" (of Beulah)'; this is explained at 62:4, where 'Beulah' (RSV mg) is the land married to God. We suggest that this is a more likely translation than the RSV attempts, both in the text and in the mg. The whole idea is observable in Jesus' evaluation of this remarkable concept of justice; at Matt. 25:21 he declares, 'Well done, good and faithful servant . . . enter into the joy of your master'. So here, 'I will faithfully give them their wages' (author's translation).

The word 'double' applied at Isa. 61:7 to Israel's portion is
not the same as that used at 40:2, although both terms mean
'twice as much'. Such then is the justice of God, understood as
the unwarranted outpouring of grace. Instead of the 'shame' of
the Exile (61:7) Israel will inherit (from God!) 'eschatological'
joy, joy on earth that has total meaning for eternity. This is
because 'my Covenant', says God, is 'everlasting', so that it too
belongs both to time and to eternity. That is why the Old Covenant is now renewed to meet the needs of the New Israel; it is
so that all may see 'that they are a people whom the LORD has
blessed' — forever (see Rom. 4:13-22). TI believed, in line with
the Torah, that a blessing mattered; it was not the uttering of
mere idle words. It conveyed the potency of the living God. Consequently, justice would be *seen* to be done once Israel's priesthood became visible to the eyes of the world.

The First Magnificat (10)

Zion speaks, acknowledging that God has now done to that community that which comprised the content of his 'mission' as described above. Zion's whole being (*nephesh*) 'rejoices', not about
some 'thing', nor that something is to happen, but 'in my God'.
God had now put his own name upon Zion (see Isa. 62:2-4).
New clothing represented a new status before God (Zech. 3:3-5;
cf. Ps. 132:9, 16; Isa. 59:17) resulting from Zion's having been
chosen for the 'mission' described at 61:3. 'The garments of salvation (*yesha'*)' revealed to all eyes that God had 'saved' their
wearer. 'He has covered me with the robe of righteousness (*tsedaqah*)': It was he who put this garment on me, not I myself.
Without him I could not have known how to love and care for
the gentile world, and so for the poor of human society.

Unlike the 'Greek' perception, followed today by a number
of Christian deviations, TI regards 'man', the generic 'person',
as being one whole. He or she is not a body within which a soul
happens to dwell. So here we notice how God 'clothes' the whole
person — body, soul, and spirit — with 'the garments of salvation';
and as this is something which God does and not humanity, and
since 'man' is free to throw off the garment as unwanted and still
remain 'man', what we are given to see is God's act of prevenient,
all-embracing grace.

'As a bridegroom decks himself' (or, with the Hebrew, 'priests

himself beautifully' in preparation for his task in the royal covenantal priesthood — that is, as he puts on the appropriate finery
for his task as priest) . . . so the LORD has dealt with Israel (cf.
John 2:1-11; Matt. 9:15).

11 Israel is to be the 'garden', or the vineyard, of the LORD —
well-kept, fruitful, a witness to all the nations (and not producing
poisonous grapes, as Isaiah had felt it necessary to say at 5:1-7).
Within the garden, however, the seed must first fall into the
ground and die (42:9; 43:19; 55:10). It is the LORD who will sow
it and let the seed 'die', as Israel did indeed 'die' in the Exile
(Ezekiel 37). However, that cannot be the end, since God is the
living God who alone can make the seed germinate. 'The Lord
GOD will cause *tsedaqah* (love by mankind for mankind) and praise
(love by mankind for God) to spring forth before all the nations'
when they turn round and look towards this chosen people, now
wearing the clothing of love, as beautiful as a garden of flowers.
This vision will necessarily become reality, because God has said
it will.

CHAPTER 62

THE NEW ISRAEL
Isaiah 62:1-12

1 What tension the author or authors of TI must have lived under. Most commentators believe that Isaiah 62 follows directly from ch. 61. If this is the case, then this speaker must have undergone a formidable revulsion of heart and mind from the high vision expressed in 61:10-11. He had only to look around him to be overwhelmed with despondency at the actual state of affairs in ruinous Jerusalem, as we know the situation to have been from the book of Haggai. Minority groups of persons with economic influence and financial power had now got together, it seems, or were beginning to coalesce in order to build elegant homes for themselves despite the ruins. They remind one today of those who are personally satisfied to have built a fallout shelter in their garden in case of nuclear war, or of those who suppose that their soul is 'saved' when the rest of society is in spiritual decay.

There was plenty of building material lying at hand for them to use, since there were bricks, stones, and rubble everywhere, and enough wood to panel their new homes comfortably on the inside (Hag. 1:4). This economically powerful group had thus sought selfishly to create themselves as the new upper class of Jerusalem's citizens. At the same time the ordinary folk, having no financial backing, were now daily going out of the city to try to work the rough ground outside, seeking evidently with scant success to bring the soured land back into fertility. Above all, inflation was upsetting the cost of living (v. 6). On the one hand, from a reading of Haggai alone one might receive the impression that that prophet took the superstitious view that God had not blessed his people merely because they had not begun to rebuild the temple. On the other hand, our author sees here that the issue is very much deeper. He is aware of the huge discrepancy that lay between the actual situation and the eschatological hope which he had preached on the previous sabbath. For it was at this juncture upon the Return from exile that eschatology, though present in seed from the earlier prophets, was now becoming central to the theology of thoughtful persons. Their thinking had been stimulated by the fact of the jubilee year that had been actuated by Cyrus when he 'redeemed' Israel exactly fifty years after the nation's 'death' in 587. They were now seeing his action as the trigger that interpreted the completion of the seventh day of creation (Isa. 61:2).

Who then is speaking here? Of course it is a human being, a poet, one who has returned from Babylon. But is this 'I' really the voice of God, or of a very confused individual? Reading on, we begin to feel that the thoughts we meet with are indeed God's thoughts, as a poor, confused poet-preacher seeks to understand and express them.

Why was Jerusalem set on a hill at all, no matter whether that city was rebuilt or not? We remember that within just one verse of the NT (Matt. 5:14) Jesus says two things: 'You are the light of the world', and 'A city set on a hill cannot be hid'. These two ideas our poet here has in mind those many centuries before Christ, but to understand them we must depart from the RSV rendering of Isa. 62:1b. We are to read instead: 'until (the fact of) God's redemption of her (his *tsedeq*) goes forth as brightness'. That sentence, however, is but one-half of the story. The other is: 'and her saving love for others (feminine *yeshu'ah*) burns like a lamp' (cf. Ps. 37:6). We are to keep in mind that there are always the two sides to God's re-creative act. The first is that which he performs in order to redeem or rescue his people — and in this case is now past history. But second, now that his act of *tsedeq* is complete, God is offering to empower his people to act in love to others in their turn. All the key words in this important verse actually go back to the preaching of Isaiah and DI (e.g., 30:15; 52:7-9). Thus it is only when 'Jerusalem' (the redeemed people) shines forth (cf. 60:3) in love to all the world that it will be seen as a city set on a hill (2:3). And never mind the bricks and mortar lying around before the poet's gaze; these are merely the facts of life in a fallen world.

2 In OT times 'a new name' was given to a person to explain and to declare his new status (cf. Gen. 32:28), as it is today in many countries of the Third World. God had promised Isaiah (Isa. 1:26) that one day he would give Jerusalem a new name. Our poet would know of Jeremiah's subsequent and similar declarations (Jer. 33:16) where the city's new name was to be 'The LORD is our righteousness' (RSV) or better, 'Yahweh is our Redeemer' (cf. Ezek. 48:35).

3 'You', then says God himself, addressing the New Israel, 'shall be a crown of beauty . . . a royal diadem in the hand of your God'.

4 Whilst Israel was in exile they had believed themselves to be 'forsaken' by God (54:6), and the Holy Land to be 'desolate'. But that unhappy situation is now evidently at an end (vv. 4-6). Says God again, 'You shall be called My delight is in her'. But *hephets* means more than mere 'delight'. What delights God is his choice of Israel, chosen as that people is for the redemption of the world. So now God himself will place that purpose of his 'in her'; that is to say, his purpose is to work out—in and through Zion and nowhere else—what today we call evidence of God's particularistic plan of love. That purpose we learned about in ch. 61. At 61:8 we already heard God say: 'I hate the rape of *Beulah* (the transliteration of the Hebrew word for 'married')'.

We cannot help but compare Isaiah 62, written in ecstatic poetry, with Ezekiel's vision of the restored Jerusalem, temple, and land, written in prose and described in a series of very pedestrian blueprints (Ezekiel 40–48). But then Ezekiel wrote before God's act of 'resurrection' had taken place through which he created the New Israel, Israel that had now been born again. Experiencing existentially in his own bones God's act of grace and renewal, TI therefore is able to go beyond Ezekiel's vision and speak ecstatically of the theological *significance* of the city of God. So at Isa. 60:1 he had said: 'Your light *has come*'. Again, Ezekiel had limited the possession of holiness to the self-righteous group of priests, the Zadokites. TI now knows that God's holiness has been granted to the whole of his people Israel.

In other words, the new name that Israel is to bear must represent to the nations of the earth what God has now done for his people, in that they have been forgiven and empowered 'to do unto others what God has done to them'. Israel's new name therefore will in some way proclaim to all peoples what their calling is as the instrument of the redeeming love of God. For just as a bride takes the name of her husband, so shall Israel take the name of her divine Husband (v. 4).

The Christian reader of the OT should take note of a reality at this point that prejudice and inherited presuppositions may have prevented him from grasping. It is that the New Israel begins its existence at this point in history, and not in the NT period. Nowhere in the Gospels do we find Jesus recognizing anything else. 'Jesus did not found a church', theologians say today, 'he found one'. And nowhere in his letters does Paul ever say that it is the Church which is really the New Israel — for Paul was a Hebrew of the Hebrews. What he does say is that the Church had now become the Israel of the New *Covenant*, in this way agreeing with Jeremiah's great outlook expressed at Jer. 31:33. And even then Paul is only saying that the new covenant is but the renewal of the ancient (*palaios*, a word which does *not* mean 'outdated') covenant that God had made with Israel through Moses (2 Cor. 3:14). If God's action in Christ remains valid forwards in time to our day, then it has been equally valid backwards to the period through which TI lived (cf. John 8:58).

The last two verses of this section contain an ecstatic mixture of metaphors, each of them conveying a most attractive picture, yet none of them taken alone being able to offer us a clear and logical theme. We are to remember, however, that throughout history the poets have often been able to express the meaning of things more decisively than the precise scientific theologian can. Our writer was a theologian who well knew the potency of the imagery of the divine marriage first expressed by Hosea and added to by Jeremiah and Ezekiel. Zion is to be given a new name, one 'which the mouth of the LORD', not 'will give' as RSV, but 'hammered out' as the Hebrew verb actually means. Does this action describe a long, hard task, as when the divine Artisan gradually creates something new out of the old? Zion is to be a beautiful 'crown'. 'And', meaning, 'that is to say', Zion is to become 'a royal diadem' in the LORD'S hand. Why does he hold it in his hand? Is it because God alone is king? We recall that 'hand' can be a metaphor for 'power'. Is it then that God is about to place the crown on Zion's head to enable her to realize she will become his powerful instrument of love? Or is Zion, God's spouse, to be acknowledged as his queen? Yet 'diadem' can mean not only a royal tiara but also the high priest's turban. The high priest was, of course, the representative to God in person of the 'kingdom of priests' (Exod. 19:6), the name given to the covenant people at Sinai. Are we then hearing about the renewal of the Covenant?

The feminine singular continues: Thou, Zion, 'shall no more be termed Forsaken'. The RSV capitalizes 'Forsaken', which suggests that this might be Zion's old name, the city that God had abandoned to destruction at the hand of Nebuchadnezzar (cf. Isa. 54:6-7; 60:15). But parallel with this we read: 'And your land shall no more be termed Desolate'. The imagery here, based as it is upon 54:6-7, confuses the two feminine entities, Zion and the land. At 54:5, when we read 'your Maker is your husband', we are presented with a reference to the city. But in the next verse the reference can only be to Zion, now personifying Israel 'like a wife forsaken . . . like a wife of youth'. This is the language of Hosea, who speaks of the divine Husband as having wooed Israel in the early days of the wilderness wanderings (Hos. 2:14-16), when Israel was still a teenage girl. Yet, Isa. 62:4 continues, the land that was 'desolation' (rather than RSV 'Desolate') — waste, negation, like the primal chaos of Gen. 1:2 — is to receive new life as a result of being 'Married' to God. For that is what marriage entails. In marriage husband and wife become one flesh (2:24). Incarnational language such as this cannot be dismissed as 'mere poetry', but must be engaged sincerely by the biblical theologian.

One further declaration unites Zion, the People of God, and the land, the 'heritage' (or perhaps the 'dowry') of the LORD (Isa. 63:17; Jer. 12:14; cf. Deut. 4:21). That declaration embodies the phrases 'My delight is in her' (Zion?) and 'your land shall be married' (author's translation) — despite the strong declaration of DI at Isa. 54:5-6, 'your Maker is your husband' — followed by 'the LORD delights in thee' (Zion?) and 'thy land shall be married'. It is the land this time, not the People of God, whom God will marry! Interestingly enough, the LXX translates 'land' here by *oikumene*, meaning literally 'inhabited' by the People of God!

However, we must bring the criteria of modern logic to solve the problem of these mixed metaphors. Our poet's whole series of images is seeking to declare that God is now actually promising a new covenant. This covenant will not be with the 'souls' of individuals amongst his people (there is no 'saving of souls' in the OT) but with his beloved partner, Israel, as a whole, renewed through having been forgiven and altogether joined up with the physical environment. (In D. W. Torrance, ed., *The Witness of the Jews to God*, 41, we see how God has used this Semitic way of thinking in connection with the Resurrection of Jesus. And we note conversely that in an atheistic and Marxist society, 'environmentalist' groups are forbidden to raise questions against state decisions.)

5 Finally, after using the analogy of sheer joy that a young man experiences when he marries, or becomes one with, his virgin bride, our poet declares that this is how the young men of Jerusalem will feel about Zion. Men and women who are members of the Covenant are to marry in order to serve the world together in the joy of the LORD. This moving idea was, of course, carried on into the thinking of the Church in the Middle Ages when it spoke also of both men and women being 'married' to Christ. The bridegroom's exultation here, however, is but a human illustration of something almost too wonderful even for poetry to express, 'thy God's' exultation 'over thee', the bride. What we learn is that it is not only Jerusalem which is to exult, God himself will exult in his saving act of union with Zion. This then is that joy of the LORD of which the whole Bible speaks (e.g., 51:11; Matt. 25:21).

Yet we must note that many commentators would understand 'your sons' to be 'your builders', with no change in the Hebrew consonants (cf. NEB), even although the LXX agrees with the MT. The LXX reads: 'As a young man sets up house with a virgin, so shall thy sons "indwell" ' (cf. Eph. 3:17; in fact, Paul seems to have taken some of his imagery from this whole passage). However, the plural of the verb in 'your sons marry you' (Isa. 62:5b) may have arisen merely by attraction from the plural of the noun for God (*elohim*) in v. 5d. So we might read here: 'Thy Rebuilder will marry thee' (cf. Ps. 147:2).

In this connection God 'built' Adam's rib into a woman (Gen. 2:22). The poet John Donne was right when he wrote: 'No man is an island entire of itself; every man is a piece of the Continent, a part of the main'. Paul, with the book of Isaiah in his heart,

could thus write: 'For we know that if the earthly tent we live in
is destroyed [the walls of which keep us separate from each other],
we have a building from God, a house not made with hands,
eternal in the heavens' (2 Cor. 5:1). 'Your builder', then, can only
be Yahweh; and as we learn from 2 Sam. 7:12-14, one 'builds a
house' by having children (Ps. 147:2). In fact, the Hebrew words
for 'build' and 'son-daughter' derive from the same root (*b-n-h*).
The picture is of God's promise of a united fellowship of men
and women, who within the 'covenant of marriage' are becoming,
through grace, the bride of God (cf. Eph. 5:25-27; Rev. 19:7).

God Speaks (6-9)

In order to establish his 'delight' (that is, his plan), not in heaven
but in the very earthy city of Jerusalem, God had 'appointed', it
seems (rather than 'set'), 'watchmen'. Their task was to watch
for the dawn (cf. Isa. 21:11-12), for the light arising that has
been mentioned at 60:1-2. The Talmud uses the term in the spe-
cialized sense of angels. But here, God himself speaking, we learn
that God had actually appointed human beings to stand on Jerusalem's 'walls'. They must 'never be silent'. 'Woe to me if I do
not preach the gospel' — did Paul get his wording from here?
(1 Cor. 9:16). The watchmen's task is to remind God of his own
nature as love! Yet, remembering that we are 'seeing' theology
through the eyes of a Semitic poet and not those of a Plato who
chose to think in abstractions, we may well suppose that the
watchman was both man and angel at once, even as he appeared
to be to the women at the empty tomb (Matt. 28:5; Mark 16:5).
The watchmen are 'never silent', 'day' or 'night'. Therefore, 'you'
too, TI declares to his congregation, must never be silent, but
ceaselessly 'put the LORD in remembrance'.

The Hebrew word *mazkir* describes a court official whose task
was to help keep a record of events and then to show them to the
king as soon as they were written down (2 Sam. 8:16; Isa. 36:3).
It was as if this royal servant almost made himself a nuisance to
his king, constantly nudging him and insisting he read what he
as 'recorder' had written down. In fact, he behaved in the manner
of the woman we know of as 'the importunate widow' (Luke
18:1-8). But then, as Jesus declared, that woman won her case!
So Jerusalem's sons (Isa. 62:5) — people (the nouns and verbs are
now plural), not bricks and mortar — are to belabour God with

the prayer (cf. Lam. 2:18) that 'thy kingdom come . . . on earth as it is in heaven'. They dare do so, knowing that God has already 'sworn by his right hand and by his mighty arm' (uplifted when making an oath) that he will certainly fulfil his promise within space and time. We recall that his hand or arm represented his stooping down into the realm of our human life on earth and acting therein.

Jerusalem, then, is to be 'a praise in the earth', that is, an object on account of which praise is offered to God. And when its people eat within it, they too shall 'praise the LORD' — as if, we might suggest, they were saying 'grace before meat' on behalf of all mankind.

Jacob Neusner points out that the Mishnah, written long after temple worship had ended in A.D. 70, wanted no more than to preserve what had survived out of the disorderly past (*Max Weber Revisited: Religion and Society in Ancient Judaism*, 21). It seeks, he declares, 'the perfection of a world at rest, the precondition of that seal of creation's perfection sanctified by the seventh day of creation'. Thus since there is no mention in Isaiah 62 of the need to rebuild the temple, as there is in Haggai, we may presume that this sermon was preached before 520 B.C., the year when Haggai appears.

The Holy People (10-12)

TI now answers the question at issue, 'What is God doing with us now that we have been rescued from the Babylonian Exile?' He answers first in terms of mission — in other words, of Israel's very *raison d'etre* within the Covenant (cf. 49:6). Israel must forget their own problems, go out through the broken-down gates of Jerusalem, and build a road on which the peoples of the earth may tread when on their way up to Zion. Too often people of little faith denounce 'foreign missions' on the ground that at home we have not yet put our own house in order. Not so, says this sermon. 'Go out into the highways and byways' and bring in 'the peoples', for it is God's plan that they should help you build a city whose name will be 'Sought out, a city not forsaken'. Thus the answer comes in terms of eschatology. For TI assumes that no matter how evil the world is, out of that 'chaos' God will 'bring up' to Zion all the humanity whom he has made in his likeness.

'Behold, the LORD has proclaimed it to the end of the earth'; this phrase occurs actually twenty-nine times in the second half of the book of Isaiah. What actually has he proclaimed? 'Behold your salvation comes.' It comes as if in its own 'person', as if salvation were now personalized and active like the angel of the LORD in ch. 63. Is it any wonder then that later writers could take the next step of using the name 'Isaiah' (*Yesha'yahu* — the name of the whole book), meaning 'The LORD is Saviour', when speaking of Jesus? Indeed, they associated the name Joshua (*ye-hoshua'*) with that of 'Jesus', for both of these names mean 'The LORD is Saviour' (Matt. 1:21).

For 'his reward is with him', as God had said to Abraham (Gen. 15:1), Israel's reward being a 'down payment of wages' paid in advance before they are even earned. This reward was God's own presence in person, *now,* as a foretaste of what is to come. Israel shall then bear their new name of 'The holy people'. This actual title occurs nowhere else in the OT; yet it is now promised to the New Israel. It does not describe those who search for an individualistic spirituality, as the Hindu Vedas demand of their readers or as is popular amongst some Christians today. Rather, it describes those who forget themselves and, leaving the safety of the city, go outside its walls and gates, 'emptying' themselves in creative love for those still outside in the realm of 'chaos'. Seeing this happen, the nations will thereupon 'seek you out'.

CHAPTER 63

GOD STOOPS TO CONQUER
Isaiah 63:1-19

1-2 The question now arises: If Yahweh is himself salvation, then how does he act to save? For example, does he act out of 'heaven', by issuing a divine fiat from on high like a Greek god?

Our poet offers us in this chapter a profound answer to this most basic of all questions — and does it in poetry too! Even Paul did not attempt to write in poetry to the church in Philippi, though he quoted poetry to make the same point as TI does here. What then is TI's description of God in his saving love, as he reveals his acts to the human eye? (This last phrase necessarily employs human language.) Remembering that God can act only in conformity with himself, throughout the OT God is shown to act in a 'passionate and aggressive concern for justice in the midst of conflict' (M. C. Lind, *Yahweh is a Warrior*, 169). Yet the human mind can grasp this reality only in terms of human warfare, so our poet takes up his theme on the basis of what he had before him in ch. 34 and 43:3.

Our typical questioner asks (63:1) 'Who is this that *has come* from Edom, in crimsoned garments from Bozrah?' The verb speaks of completed action, not as the RSV rendering, because God's redemption is already complete. These lines are, of course, an allusion to 34:6-7. Edom, to the southeast of the Holy Land, with Bozrah its chief town, was believed to be the homeland of the descendants of Esau (see Gen. 36:8). Esau, the brother of Jacob, was he who cared so little for God's Covenant and for his own birthright within it, that he sold the latter to Jacob for a mess of pottage (25:29-34). Thereafter, down the centuries Israel had regarded the craftiness of Jacob to be a mere peccadillo in comparison with Esau's contemptuous rejection of his calling to work with God in covenant for the redemption of the world, as

70

well as Edom's continued contempt for his brother-nation Israel (Amos 1:11-12). This became conspicuous especially after Nebuchadnezzar had destroyed Jerusalem in 586 (Ps. 137:7). At that crisis Edom had simply walked in and looted and destroyed amongst the ruins (Isa. 34:5-17; Ezek. 25:12; 35; 36:5-7; Obad. 13-14, 16).

Now, the name Edom means 'red', and the name Bozrah means 'vintager', one who treads out the grapes with his feet. Thus we are being shown right from the first line that we are dealing not with a parable, for a parable makes only one point, but with an issue that can be understood 'by the human eye' — one that is applicable, in the particularistic manner of the Bible, to just one nation yet at the same time to the whole world of mankind. We recall that for Isaiah, Israel is God's vine situated in his chosen vineyard (Isa. 5:1-7; cf. Ps. 80:8). Thus it is in Israel that God is 'trampling out the vintage where the grapes of wrath are stored' (in the words of Julia Ward Howe's great hymn). But at the same time we discover that it is out of this 'holocaust' (and *not* 'from heaven') that Yahweh has here emerged.

We note a further point. Not only is Edom red, but so too is 'Man'. The name Adam employs in Hebrew the same consonants as does Edom. For since in biblical times Hebrew possessed no vowels, the three consonants composing this word could be read both ways. We recall that when God 'formed man of dust from the ground' (Gen. 2:7), he formed him from the red sandstone soil of Palestine and the Arabian peninsula. The ancient Israelites did not think of themselves as being white skinned, as do Europeans today, nor even as pink, as the Chinese regard the Caucasian. So while the poem clearly refers to Edom because of the name Bozrah coupled with it, it refers at the same time to all mankind. We may go further, and see that Edom may be equivalent to the name Babylon, just as in the NT Babylon became a figure for Rome (cf. Ps. 137:7-8). If such is the case, then in 'announcing vindication, mighty to save', the reference is to more than when God rescued Israel from Babylon; it must refer also to God's plan to rescue all mankind and vindicate them by his love and justice—for God does not change (Mal. 3:6).

We have learned from DI that God was 'in Israel' in his saving love; that is, he was present in his covenant people (Isa. 45:14-15). He had thus 'clothed himself with his Servant people.' Here TI describes God as 'glorious in his apparel' or, literally, 'swelling in his clothing', wearing Israel as a king shows his majesty, his royal strength, by his glorious apparel.

Now, God's covenant was not with Jacob alone; Esau too was a son of the covenant that God had made with Abraham. Esau might deliberately choose to ignore his responsibilities within it, but God does not forget his promises, for God is faithful; his *hesed* can be described as 'I will never let you go' (Psalm 136). God could say: 'I have loved Jacob but I have hated Esau' (Mal. 1:2-3). But that does not mean that he has let Esau go. Israel he could and did use; Esau he did not use — yet he remained faithful to Esau. But even Israel had now failed God and had needed to be 'educated' by means of the sorrows of the Exile. So God had now been left alone. Israel, his 'garment', God had been forced to lay aside, so that when he was treading the grapes of wrath he was all alone and wore only his own 'crimsoned garments'.

The answer to the question put in Isa. 63:1 comes ringing back: 'It is I, mighty to save'. Modern people like to speak of God as the Almighty. TI sees his nature otherwise. For him, God is rather Almighty Love. Moreover, the answer comes through the spoken Word here expressed by an active participle, to show that God is always saving through his love.

The RSV translation 'vindication' needs clarification. For the word is not the masculine *tsedeq* we have noticed so often used to describe God's act of redemption. It is the feminine *tsedaqah*, which portrays the effect of God's action in the lives of those he has redeemed, rendering them loving and creative personalities the one toward the other.

Note therefore that the questioner does not see the Saviour God as a war-god, a Roman Mars marching to victory over the bodies of the slain.

3-6 The word 'march' (*tsa'ah*) in v. 1 can mean two things, and in the true Hebraic manner here it surely means both at once. First, it does indeed mean 'to march', even as a soldier marches; but there is no description here of a battle between warriors. Second, it means 'to stoop'. The God who 'treads in the wine press' is the one who stoops to conquer, who like the Suffering Servant of Isaiah 53 empties himself to win the victory. It is he who has stooped to enter the wine press, the 'holocaust' of blood and horror, and who has borne the whole weight of his redemptive work on his own stooping shoulders. What we are to realize is that the nations have made life for each other on this planet hell on earth, but that God has chosen to handle their folly by letting them see the effect upon himself of the hellishness of their behaviour. God sees that, although he is mighty in his strength (v. 1c), he has no more powerful way to redeem the peoples than by immersing himself in their bloody activities. TI thus makes crystal clear that God does not save 'from above', by remaining impassive and remote; he does so by walking beside the prisoners in the burning fiery furnace (Dan. 3:25; cf. Isa. 43:2), by descending into Edom (or Babylon), or by sharing the horrors of an 'Auschwitz' with his own beloved people. The challenge to do this was terrible for even God to contemplate. He had to 'lean on' his own passion (*hemah*) to bring him through. So it was that 'my wrath upheld me' (63:5), in the light of 59:16, where we learned that God saw the necessity of acting alone. When humanity creates a Bozrah or an Auschwitz, only God can do something about it. On the other hand, ch. 63 makes staggeringly clear that the demonic in God is an absolutely necessary part of his being and activity, else his saving love could not reach down to where evil exists even lower than mankind can reach (Deut. 32:39; 1 Sam. 2:6; Isa. 45:7; Amos 3:6).

In plain language, then, what this passage is saying is that God's righteous vengeance upon sinners takes the form of his acting to redeem them and to save them from their various hells. This is how Zechariah interprets this theological reality a generation or two later: 'Because of the blood of my covenant with you, I will set your captives free' (Zech. 9:11; cf. Exod. 24:8; Mark 14:24; Heb. 9:20-22). In his *Church Dogmatics* Karl Barth expresses TI's vision in stern language, seeing here 'the abyss on whose edge . . . every man of God and every genuine prophet walks' (2/2: 399).

TI is saying that God is the victor in his war against evil, not by offering violence but by submitting to it. The prophet gives us a picture of God at a specific moment in history, as specific as A.D. 33 or 1944 (the year of Auschwitz). This is a picture of God 'going down' into the seething vat, the arena of 'man's inhumanity to man', so that even as they spill each other's blood the living God becomes soaked therewith. From their blinded view of life, mankind can discover no meaning or purpose in their own wars and bloodletting. God alone knows how to use mankind's hellish activities for good; he does so by taking upon himself the absurdity of human violence. This is so unspeakable, so 'total', that God needs the absoluteness of his own *hemah* to let him do so — especially since, being '*in* Israel', he has thereby to tread the grapes himself. So we are grateful to God that he chose to use Israel, 'my first-born son' (Exod. 4:22) as the guinea pig for all generations to come. For, being 'in Israel', he allowed himself to be defeated in 587 B.C., and to be defeated actually by 'my servant Nebuchadnezzar' (Jer. 25:9). We are grateful that the whole line of theologians in the book of Isaiah was able to wrestle through the whole issue, and so to have provided us today with a theology of God that interprets to us the cross of Christ (Matt. 16:21).

Such then is a total picture of divine grace. That it is a true revelation of grace has been questioned, of course, all down the centuries, simply because we are all sinful creatures who cannot believe that grace could be so wonderful. And so there were theologians who insisted that God must be impassible. Throughout the Scholastic period, for example, and into and beyond the Reformation the debate continued. Johannes Duns Scotus was born in the year that Thomas Aquinas produced his *Summa Theologica* (A.D. 1265). It was Duns Scotus who reaffirmed the totality of divine grace as against Thomist soteriology, as did Martin Luther and most of his followers. But then these scholars took the OT as seriously as they did the NT. Yet even today the debate goes on.

A Prophetic Liturgy (7-8)

In what at first sight looks like an independent poem we are given an exegesis of the words 'my own arm brought me victory' (v. 5c), or better, 'wrought salvation'. Today one meets with attempts at creating a theology of the Cross that takes no account of the Covenant, or even of the OT itself for that matter. But to our poet the Covenant is all-important. The two English words 'steadfast love' represent the covenantal term *hesed*. It is known to Israel as the basic experience granted them at Sinai (Exod. 20:5-6; see Psalm 136). Here the word is used in the plural, describing the loving actions created and performed by the living

God in history. I will 'recount' these, says TI, meaning bring them to mind, telling others about God's loyalty (*hesed*) and compassion (*rahamim*) or 'mercy' (RSV). This declaration of the prophet is important.

Down through the centuries there have been those who have sought God in the silence. Such silence can only too easily ignore historical facts. Dietrich Bonhoeffer notes that mystical silence, 'in its absence of words, is . . . the soul secretly chattering away to itself' (*Christ the Center*, 27). But what the OT (and the Church) demands of us 'is silence before the Word'. So here our poet has been silent; he has listened, he has read his Scriptures first, the record of God's mighty saving acts of love. Only then, therefore, does he declare: 'I will recount the steadfast love of the LORD'.

One such act of love is described in this way: 'For he said, Surely (*ak*, 'Oh, but they are not like that!'), they are my people, sons who will not deal falsely (*shaqar*)', simply because they have been my people since the days of Moses (Exod. 19:5). The next half-line is a simple statement. Knowing in his love for them that his people must live with the mystery of evil, 'he became their Savior'. His means to that end was to enter into a covenant with them.

9 Within the bonds of the Covenant, then, God shared Israel's life. So, naturally, 'in all their affliction he was afflicted'. The text of this crucial verse, however, is disputable. The Hebrew runs: 'In all their affliction he was not an adversary, and the angel of his "face" ("presence") saved them'. This phrase refers to the angel of the Covenant mentioned at Exod. 23:20-22.

'The angel of God', or 'the angel of Yahweh', or just 'the angel' appears frequently in the earlier literature. We may observe two things about him. (1) He seems to have no essential 'being' of his own; he is exactly what the word angel means, a messenger. He is like a flame of fire that obeys its master by igniting the woodpile and then disappearing (Ps. 104:4). He is of no importance in himself; what is important is the message he brings. The message in question has come forth from the mouth of God in the form of his Word (cf. Gen. 48:16). (2) The 'Word' may take the form of a human person, for the messenger usually (but not always) is made visible to human consciousness as a human being (16:7-11; Num. 22:22-35; Judg. 2:1-4; 6:11-22; 13:3-21). It

is by basing his thought on a passage such as this that John
Calvin could hold the twin theological emphases in balance, that
justification is not only *through* Christ (the 'evangelical' emphasis)
but is also *in* Christ (the 'catholic' emphasis).

We note that 'the' angel (LXX 'my' angel) knows the way to
the prepared place. Yet God's name, or person, is *in* his angel.
God gives to us human beings not a surrogate for himself but his
own self in love and pity. Israel therefore, the covenant partner,
must necessarily obey him and not rebel against him, 'for my
name is in him' (Exod. 23:21). That is, though remaining transcendent, God is at the same time present 'in person'. In the
Exodus passage we read that '*he* will not pardon your transgression', the 'he' being the angel, for it is only God who can forgive
sin (Isa. 43:11-13). TI concludes this allusion by taking up the
word *tsar* used at 63:10, 'therefore he turned to be their enemy'.

At Exod. 14:19; 23:20-22; 33:2, 14 and frequently elsewhere,
especially at Isa. 37:36, in observing the action of the angel we
see the face of the God who is beyond human sight. This perhaps
is why the LXX, feeling the need to offer a positive exegesis of
this verse from outside the Hebraic thinking of the Holy Land
(for the translation was made within the philosophical back-
ground of Hellenistic culture in Egypt), and in light of v. 5, translates: 'Not an ambassador, but himself saved them' (cf. NEB).

But why did God do so? 'Because he loved him, and he himself
redeemed them.' Then, following the covenant wording of Exod.
19:4, TI adds, 'He lifted them up and carried them all the days
of old', as an Eastern mother would carry her baby on her back
across the Sinai desert.

10-14 'But as for them (*wehemmah*), they rebelled.' That action
by Israel 'grieved his holy Spirit' or, as we might say, broke God's
heart. Verse 10b thus shows a continuity with v. 6, making the
whole chapter a unity. We read that when God was heartbroken
at the sin of humanity (Gen. 6:6) he 'remembered' Noah (8:1).
So too here, God 'remembered' how he had given Israel his Covenant and had promised to be their God no matter what might
happen.

God then even proceeds to ask himself questions! 'Where is he
who brought up . . . ?' In 'the days of old, of Moses', Miriam and
Aaron had been 'the shepherds of his flock'. In other words, God

asks himself if he had not perhaps reneged on his responsibilities to Israel within the Covenant.

'Where is he who put in the midst of them his holy Spirit (which is to be obeyed, v. 10)?' This question has worried some expositors, for nowhere in the book of Exodus is the holy Spirit ever even mentioned. But what we do find in Exodus is that Yahweh put his Word in Israel's midst at Sinai when he gave his people the Torah. Eight hundred years later, therefore, TI found no difficulty in identifying the Spirit with the Word of God. TI was thus no 'biblical literalist'. Rather, he interpreted the Scriptures as he felt them to be true, yet in accordance with the new circumstances that had developed over the years. In like manner, because he was a close disciple of the Isaiahs, Paul virtually never quoted the OT literally, but adapted his references to interpret the Word to give meaning within his still very different circumstances.

God's 'glorious arm' was his Spirit in action within space and time. Such an action occurred when God's arm became Moses' arm, as we read at Exod. 17:8-13 (see also 6:6; 15:16).

If God 'brought up out of the sea', then he had first to 'go down' himself. Either the descent was the 1200-m. (4000-ft.) drop from the mountains of Moab to the Jordan Valley before Israel could go up out of the river Jordan into the Promised Land (Exod. 33:14); or, with the LXX, the descent was into the abyss (cf. Ps. 106:9), the valley of the shadow of death, the seas of chaos as represented by the Red Sea (cf. Isa. 51:9-10). And God did all this 'to make for himself an everlasting name', that is 'for his own name's sake', since God is all in all and his love is everything. We note that he led his people '*through* the depths' (of chaos, of 'hell') without destroying chaos itself; for God actively employs chaos to re-create his world (see Isaiah 65 – 66). This renewing, re-creative love is God's *tsedaqah* for his own fallen world.

The 'name' of God is thus the description of who God is as he works out his saving plan and leads his people to that end. For he had said: 'I will be with you. . . . This is my name for ever' (Exod. 3:12, 15). At Isa. 18:7 Isaiah had called Mt. Zion 'the place of the name of the LORD of hosts'. So TI, his 'disciple' two hundred years later, is keenly conscious that it is in Jerusalem alone, to which 'thou didst lead thy people', that God's act of salvation is to take place. This is to be the salvation, not just of

Israel alone, but of all mankind. Jesus declared the same still another five hundred years later (cf. Matt. 16:21). And TI would recall that other cry of so long before, 'O LORD, we wait for thee [for] thy memorial name' (Isa. 26:8).

A Revulsion of Spirit (15-19)

But life in Jerusalem is not like that now (ca. 530 B.C.). Some seven or eight years earlier the faithful (the *tsaddiqim*) had been ordered by God to stop worrying about their own salvation, whether physical or spiritual, and turn their attention to all those who were struggling up the hill to Zion (Isa. 60:10-12; 62:10). The elect evidently had been thinking of themselves as the True Israel, as many Christian sects do even to this day; and so they were excluding from salvation all who were not of their way of thinking. They had brushed aside the Isaian awareness that to be the 'holy people' (62:12) they must reveal in their lives what God's holiness is like: 'The Holy God shows himself holy in righteousness (*tsedaqah*)' (5:16), love for others, love for all the peoples of the earth. 'You shall be holy, for I am holy', God had declared repeatedly in the Torah.

Not grasping this word of revelation, at least one of the returned priestly group now pens a whine of self-pity. God had indeed been good to Israel in the days of the Exodus, but what was he doing now? 'The yearning of thy heart' should be rendered by the much more anthropomorphic expression 'the thunder of thy bowels'. Such a phrase emphasises that God could be totally, even 'bodily', upset, or perhaps 'existentially', as we might say. Then follows the word 'compassion', 'thy motherly love' from the root for 'womb'. This phrase must therefore refer back to 49:15. Yet despite this 'motherly' figure of speech, we hear next of God as 'our Father'.

'Where are thy zeal and thy might?', zeal being *qinah*, the 'jealousy' of God mentioned in the Second Commandment. Zeal is the logical link between wrath and love (Exod. 20:5). TI handles this description of God eminently well in Isaiah 66 (see Heb. 10:27). God had promised Abraham, Israel's progenitor, that he would be the father of a great multitude (Gen. 17:5). But now this verse declares: However, it is 'thou', God, who 'art our Father' (as if he were saying 'And don't forget it!'), not 'Abraham', not Jacob ('Israel'); it is thou who art 'our Redeemer from of old'. Thou alone art our Saviour; we are not saved by any birth-right, but by grace alone. 'Abraham does not know us'; the word 'know' is used in the sense of 'beget' as in Gen. 4:1. It is Yahweh who is the God of the fathers (Exod. 3:13; Deut. 1:21; Josh. 18:3), the Father-Creator-Redeemer of his people (Jer. 3:19; 31:9; Mal. 1:6; 2:10). By saying as much our writer tells us that the purpose of human fatherhood under the divine Father is to redeem one's own children, to bring them up in the ways of God.

But this verse means more than that. We are now separated from Abraham, he is saying. Abraham was the person who, through faith, was ordained by God to become a blessing to all the families of the earth (Gen. 12:3). It seems then that 'Abraham does not know us' because we have abandoned our calling to incorporate this blessing in our lives (Isa. 49:6). In consequence God has had to act as our surrogate Father, and so he became our Saviour, 'from of old' (see v. 9). If it had not been so, we could not have become his 'servants'. For as our Redeemer, God stands between our real selves, what God's children ought to be, and our actual selves, who are 'like those who are not called by thy name', for we have given up the family name offered us by grace (cf. 65:9).

There follows a verse that enshrines a crux for biblical faith. This particular preacher had simply not absorbed in faith the mystery of God's redemptive act in 'resurrecting' his elect people from the 'death' of the Exile to new life in the elect city as the New Israel of God. Here he puts the blame on God for the be-haviour of his contemporaries. 'Why' — the eternal cry of lonely humanity — 'dost thou make us err from thy ways?' He implies that God had left Israel free to worship what is not God. (Paul deals with this issue at Rom. 1:24, 26, 28.) This is of course a perennial problem to faith. It was recognized as such by the young Isaiah at his call (Isa. 6:9-13). Jesus included the issue as a clause in the Lord's Prayer. It would have remained a problem right from the penning of the Song of Moses on into the NT, had it not been recognized by each new generation that God uses the evil to produce the good. Incidentally, we note that this speaker suggests that he and his contemporaries were not able to keep the law in their own strength; so it was God's fault for creating them the kind of people they were.

But the next phrase goes even farther. Why dost thou 'harden

our heart, so that we fear thee not?' Here the verb *qashah* is used,
the strongest of all the verbs for 'harden' that are employed in
the book of Exodus. Could it be that God was handling his redeemed people in the same way as he had handled Pharaoh of
old (Exod. 4:21), and in fact in the way he had handled the whole
Egyptian people (14:17; Josh. 11:20)? (For a discussion of this
issue, see my *Theology as Narration: A Commentary on the Book of
Exodus*, 69-72.) Was it the case, people wondered, that, while
Yahweh had indeed fetched his people home, he himself had not
returned? So we hear the cry to God: 'Return for the sake of thy
servants, the tribes of thy heritage'. 'Don't demand of us that we
should restore the old paths and keep the Torah without your
being present with us, LORD, in person! Come back and do something different for us than the strange way you have chosen.'
Here the word 'return' is a verbal imperative that can also mean
'repent'. So the speaker may be cheekily telling God to change
his ways and act more like the way a god should act!

Using the root *shub* ('repent'), the book of Isaiah can speak of
God returning to Israel (Isa. 52:8) and of Israel returning to God
(35:10; 51:11); of Israel's task to bring home the lost sheep (49:6),
and so to 'restore' the covenant continuity. God too restores in
wrath (1:25; 65:15); no one can 'bring back' his purpose (14:27)
or 'turn back' his Word from going forth. All these usages thus
show God to be the God who acts, who reveals himself only by
acting. And he expects mankind to do the same. At 44:22 God
had said 'Return to me, for I have redeemed you'. But they had
not, even though God had indeed 'returned' to Israel when he
led them home.

Finally, we are given a glimpse of the reasoning of this group.
They remind God of the days of old, first when there was the
temple of Solomon containing the 'mercy seat' (as the Hebrew
is translated), that one spot on earth where God met with humans in forgiveness and redemptive love. And then, even in exile
and the temple gone, 'thy holy people *still* possessed thy sanctuary a little while'. Walther Zimmerli translates this phrase by
'a token sanctuary', or 'a temporary sanctuary', or by 'not much
of a sanctuary' (to be sarcastic!) as Ezekiel had declared when
he was in exile (Ezek. 11:16). Perhaps Ezekiel was one of those
who brought together a handful of loyalists into what later generations, looking back, might call a 'synagogue'. But now the

people were no better off than the Gentiles, none of whom were 'called by thy name', 'Ben Yahweh' (cf. Isa. 43:7) or 'Yahweh-son', as Israel was. But whatever is the correct reading of 'a little while', the complaint points to a collapse of faith—not in God's existence, but in God's power and love. Yet Deut. 28:1-14, which would be in the hands of this priestly group, had described just how God would and must act in the situation in which they found themselves.

We should take note that nowhere in this whole chapter do we find the concept that a person's *teshubah* ('turning') can restore him to God's fellowship, such as by keeping the law or by striving after obedience. Here it is God alone who must *shub* ('return', v. 17c), in accordance with his basic loyalty and self-giving which we see to be the essence of the Covenant that he himself has imposed upon his people.

CHAPTER 64

AN AMBIVALENT FAITH
Isaiah 64:1-12

1-2   The text of the Hebrew Bible makes v. 1 the climax to the cry of despair at 63:15-19. What then does it mean? The Hebrew has: 'If only thou hadst rent the heavens and come down'. The verb here is in the past tense and so does not express a wish for the future; it is not a 'perfect tense of wish fulfilment' as some suggest. The NEB is thus correct when it translates by 'Why didst thou not rend the heavens'. So the chapter continues: Why didst thou not do something spectacular like melting the mountains, as when a great volcanic eruption sets fire to whole forests and boils up the waters of great lakes? If only thou hadst done so, then that would have made 'thy name known to thy adversaries . . . that the nations might tremble at thy presence'. This is exactly the kind of thinking prevalent today. 'Give me just one proof of the existence of God.' 'I cannot believe, without tangible scientific evidence, as I would in the case of a forest fire or a volcanic eruption.' Or, with Jesus, 'If they do not hear Moses and the prophets, neither will they be convinced if some one should rise from the dead' (Luke 16:31).

Our author, having in mind his inherited awareness of God as *elohim* (a plural noun) was not worried, as his Gentile counterpart might have been, to suppose that any 'coming down' of God—any humiliation or shrinking of the state of God—would make God any less the God he knew as *elohim*. There is room in the plurality and complexity of God's Being for just such a divine eventuality, as DI, our author's mentor, had shown him. For God had 'come down' to share with his Servant Israel the humiliation, suffering, and death of the Exile in Babylon (Isaiah 53). Before that time God had never proved his divinity by 'coming down' in earthquakes, wind, or fire (cf. Elijah's experience at 1 Kgs.

19:11-12) — in other words, in some great and mighty theophany. On the other hand, he had long since made himself known to Moses' people as he continued to keep the promise he made at the burning bush: 'I AM', or better, ' "I will be" with you' (Exod. 3:12). No wonder the awesomeness of that promise had struck sheer terror into the heart of Isaiah. He had exclaimed: 'Who among us can dwell with the devouring fire?' (Isa. 33:14); 'It will be sheer terror to understand the message' (28:19).

To apply the words 'come down' to God implies that he must first be 'up there' or, to use our modern jargon, that God is transcendent. But 'down here', without God, there is only meaninglessness. Though without transcendence our human life would not exist as life at all, it is only with God's 'coming down' that mankind can discover who God really is. Isaiah had known that since Moses' day God had never ceased to 'come down', for Isaiah was able to speak of God as Immanuel (8:8), meaning 'God is with us, here, at hand'. So TI could declare that God's name was *in* 'the angel of his presence' (63:9). But most potently of all, he could declare that God was *in* Israel (45:14) as DI had taught him while they were both together in Babylon.

Thou Didst Terrible Things (3-5a)

Yet God had indeed come down in days of old and had done 'terrible things'. The Hebrew word *noraoth* is used only of that which is humanly inexplicable, such as are all God's acts of grace. In the OT we are not concerned with 'religion' so much as with 'revelation'. The OT reaches that point, not by speculative thinking, but by building its theology upon facts of history. The basic fact the OT thinkers rely upon is the fact of Israel. And it was to this factual people that God had done 'terrible things which we looked not for', theological realities beyond any questions we might raise about the meaning of life. (Note how at 1 Cor. 2:9 Paul has developed this verse to fit the ever-evolving theology of the Scriptures.) Too often, even today, people begin their speculations on the basis of their own presuppositions about what God must be like, and not on that of the biblical revelation.

We know a great deal about the god Baal from the literature of the Canaanites; he was the god of the tempest, and he rode his chariot upon the clouds. By contrast, when Israel's God came down, 'no one heard' him speak (Isa. 64:4). All that people could see or hear was a series of natural events, such as the 'miracles' he wrought for Israel in Egypt; and such 'miracles', as the modern sceptic might say, can all be explained away. On the other hand, Yahweh is a God 'who works for those who wait for him', for those who expect to hear his voice — not in the earthquake or in the trampling of the warriors' boots, but as the still small voice uttered in the silence of the Word (as Dietrich Bonhoeffer expressed it, while awaiting his martyrdom at the will of Adolf Hitler). And so our poet now actually answers himself in faith about the God whose concern for Israel he had doubted. He comes back from his doubts by reading again the central message of Isaiah, and now comments upon it. The answer he finds is that God is love. Biblical mysticism is the other side of the coin of the ethic of love (61:1-3). At 51:6 DI had used the very words we find our poet quoting here. But in his verse DI had completed his apocalyptic picture with the words 'but my salvation shall be for ever'; that is to say, it belongs in eternity, and so it is something to which volcanoes and floods can merely point, since these events are not the reality in themselves.

Unfortunately the text of 64:4 is somewhat corrupt. It must have been so even in Paul's day, for that great interpreter of Isaiah, with the help of the LXX translation along with v. 5a, has given us his understanding of these lines at 1 Cor. 2:9 in immortal words, especially as we know them from the KJV:

> Eye hath not seen, nor ear heard,
> neither have entered into the heart of man,
> the things which God hath prepared for them that love him.

The love of God is apparent therefore only to 'him that joyfully works righteousness, those that remember thee in thy ways'. It is only such who are aware that God is love, this God of the thunderstorm who does terrible things. Though he is the infinitely high God, he bends down to us with a love from the higher to the lower, with a love that bridges the gap — yet which thereby confirms that there is a gap. His is love that acts freely (63:17), yet in which he gives himself fully even while remaining himself. This love is a jealous love (v. 16), for in it God shows that he really and fully wants us for himself, to accept him as 'our Father', so that he may be one with us in the exclusiveness of his divine Being. Thus it is sin and sin only that separates us from

God, while it is love and love only that is the antidote to sin. For it is only when we 'remember thee in thy ways' that we become fully aware how great the LORD is. 'We' is still inclusive ('we all') here, not just one section of Israel. 'We' is all God's people together, for all of us are sinners no matter to which sect or party we belong.

We Are All Sinners (5b-7)

Bit by bit, then, we hear our author reassembling his faith. He recognizes that God had indeed 'come down' — but in judgment upon 'our sins'. 'We have been sinners from the beginning' (or, with the LXX, 'have been rebellious' against the Covenant). How then can we be saved? In reply to this question TI declares, first, that we must not despair of being the objects of God's care. Second, we must face up to what sin actually is in the sight of the holy God. 'A polluted garment' is one that has been rendered filthy from constant menstruation (plural). But menstruation is a fact of our human situation, and not of our own will (Lev. 12:2). Over against this, TI is concerned that we are to do 'all our righteous deeds' (the RSV term) in face of our human condition, to perform acts of love (*tsedaqot*) simply because God has first acted in this manner to us.

Because of our human condition, no one 'arouses himself', as from the sleep of death, 'to take hold of thee'. Such language infers that God had indeed 'come down' sufficiently for mankind to do such a thing, that God was indeed Immanuel after all. Yet the author declares that God had 'hid thy face from us', had 'melted' us (RSV mg) into the power of our own iniquity (the Hebrew is in the singular). How vivid Hebrew metaphors can be. This one is as vivid as our English equivalent, 'God leaves us to stew in our own juice'. So here we are not far from the mystery of the hardening of the heart that TI has mentioned before.

Some commentators suggest that the word 'unclean' (v. 6) refers to the cultic state of the people, since there is no temple now in Jerusalem at which they can worship. As a result, with no sacrifices available they cannot be cleansed. This is not a likely interpretation, since it is Israel's rejection of living the life of creative, saving love that is the issue in question. In other words, 'unclean' refers to the uselessness of 'good deeds' performed outside the covenant relation to the God who gave it.

The Poet's Ambivalent Claim on God (8-12)

And 'yet, O LORD, thou art our Father'! This time the word is clearly used to mean Creator (cf. 63:16), but not it seems the Creator of free conscious beings (cf. Job 10:9; Isa. 29:16; Jeremiah 19). Clay can only perform what the hand makes it do. What we have here then is a thoroughgoing predestination expressed in terms of Isa. 64:6-7 but in contradistinction to vv. 4-5. Yet it would be unjust to press this imagery as far as that. What is probably behind TI's metaphor is a demand upon God not to let the potter's wheel cease turning, but that God should complete the artifact he had begun to fashion — in this case, his own chosen people. Thus, 'remember not iniquity for ever' may not be the best reading of the line. Both the LXX and the Dead Sea Scrolls text have read *la'et* for *la'ad,* thus meaning 'in season' instead of 'for ever'. At 61:2 we heard that the 'season' of God's redemptive activities had come. Perhaps the speaker here is reminding God of this fact. But he is also saying, 'Consider, LORD, we are all thy people', a mixed bunch of good and bad — yet perhaps not so bad after all — certainly not bad enough to bring down upon us such anger as thou has shown (cf. Lam. 4:6).

To experience the full life, human beings need to live in communities. But 'thy holy cities have become a wilderness' — that is to say, all the towns of Judah and Samaria where the worship of Yahweh had once been carried on — especially 'Jerusalem', called here by its theological title of 'Zion'. Within it the temple, God's 'holy and beautiful house', where 'our fathers' used to praise thee, 'has been burned by fire'. What can God mean, the prophet must have pondered, if Israel's God (of love!) had allowed such a blasphemous event to take place. And all our ancient 'pleasant places' — public buildings and stately homes — 'have become ruins'.

So we watch our theologian-poet struggling to make sense of his faith. He has not yet reached the point of declaring to his congregation that believers must not try to live by mere subjective assurance, or by declaring that God always answers prayer as we expect him to. Rather, he is struggling to discover that it is enough to recognize only what God has *done,* in and through his mighty acts. It is imperative then that the Israel of 530 B.C. should live by that faith, even if the prophet himself still has his doubts. In the same way, we are witnessing today the rejection of the biblical faith by the peoples of the West, especially the faith that the cross of Christ is the final and valid *act* of God in his redemptive plan. For as people today take note, obviously the world is not saved. Facing such a challenge to faith, a private, subjective experience of salvation is not the answer, although it undoubtedly points towards that answer. How very important this whole chapter is then, as its author wrestles with the meaning of faith in a manner that has universal application, in our day as well as his.

TI seems to be fighting not just the enemy within himself, but also the preconceptions, as he sees them, of some of his contemporaries. Undoubtedly some of the Levites had never been removed into exile and had continued to minister to the peasants in Palestine over the years. Now, with Haggai and Zechariah, they would want to rebuild the temple, to 'start again just where we left off'. They were able to do nothing but exteriorize religion, for they had learned nothing from history. They had not been 'there' in the 'burning fiery furnace' of the Exile, and so could not understand the significance of DI's theological interpretation of that event (43:2). And so they were not able to grasp the outcome of it, the 'resurrection' of the dry bones of those who had suffered in that foreign land. Theologians today speak of the falsity of trying to do theology in 'antiseptic laboratories'. TI knew better. He was now labouring, even as his heart was torn in two, to understand the strange ways of God in the rotting ruins of the once beautiful city known before as 'the joy of all the earth' (Lam. 2:15).

What a paradoxical God this is, however, to whom our author is appealing. Down the centuries he had disclosed himself to Israel through the utterance of his Word. But now God himself, it seems, had created the basic stumbling-block to faith, so that a sincere, believing man must exclaim: 'Wilt thou keep silent, and afflict us sorely?' Why should God not now burst forth with a miracle and restore Jerusalem to its former glory? But now TI had come to see that God is not like that. The clearer God reveals himself, the thicker must be the disguise he adopts. The more penetrating the question of God's providence and plan, the more impenetrable must be his incognito. Unless this were so, of course, Israel would not live by faith but by sight. If God had performed such a miracle as some hoped for, then his act would not have been a miracle, it would have been just magic. Magic is something that belongs only within the realm of space and time, and is not part of eternity. If God had thus practised magic or spoken through astrological pronouncements, nothing would have happened to the returned exiles. They would have remained merely the same perversely unclean and unrighteous group as they had been the day they came home from Babylon (Isa. 64:6). So we discover that TI, and with him the people of Israel, still has very much to learn about grace and about the unimaginably great purposes of God.

CHAPTER 65

GOD'S REPLY
Isaiah 65:1-25

1-5 Paul, in his day, lived in a society that was religiously divided just as were the people who were now resettling themselves in Jerusalem. Because of this, it is clear that Paul made himself aware of the contents of this chapter.

The evidence of the early chapters of Ezra is that, in proportion to the availability of homes in the ruined city, quite large numbers of loyal, believing people — both clergy and laity — had by now (probably some years after Isaiah 64 was preached) returned from Babylon. No wonder, as Haggai angrily declares, (Hag. 1:4), these settlers had had to spend so much of their energies on merely getting settled. But there were evidently others also in Jerusalem — adventurers, drifters, men and women with no home roots who knew nothing of national boundaries, just like the modern Bedouin. These were an easy prey to the superstitions of the peasantry who, for the past fifty years, had mingled with the Canaanite population. Isaiah 65 therefore now takes up issues raised at 64:8-12, while vv. 3-5 take up what was said at 57:5-13. This is all expressed in a divine speech in reply to the lament uttered in the previous chapter.

As the stream of returnees grew in number, says God, 'I spread out my hands all the day (or 'everyday') to a rebellious people'. 'I said, "Here am I, here am I" ' — 'close beside you', 'Immanuel'. Such a cry reveals therefore the amazing humility of the living God. Paul is so struck by it that he quotes it at Rom. 10:20-21 (cf. Ezek. 14:3; 20:3, 31). 'People' here is the word *goy*; God's usual term for his own people is *'am*. But he is now faced with the problem of having to deal out of sheer grace with a people that has placed itself outside of the Covenant he had given them in the days of Moses. Thus the words 'A nation that did not call on my name' could equally well be vowelled to read 'were not called by my name'; that is, they no longer used the name of the divine Husband. It was this lapsed house of Israel, then, that God was patiently waiting to 'ask for me'! In fact, the tables are turned here. To 'spread out the hands' is the position that a person takes when he seeks God in prayer. But here it is God who spreads out his hands to mankind! This means that we learn from God himself that the One who does 'terrible things' (64:3) is also the One who is utterly humble before mankind. How astonishing is this Isaian picture of God's love.

At 55:6 we heard the gracious call of God to his people *before* they had been released by Cyrus: 'Seek the LORD while (or 'where') he may be found, call upon him while (or 'where') he is near'. But now that they had been granted freedom and were back at home in Jerusalem, these same people had thereupon lost interest in God's initial act of *tsedeq*. Being rebels, the technical term for covenant-breakers, they had rejected the God who had chosen them in love — an issue to be kept in mind by all those who today espouse a 'liberation theology'. They were not prepared to make a response to God's renewed initiative, and 'couldn't care less' about God's plans for his city (64:8-12). Moreover, they had been heard to sneer at the Mosaic legislation, saying 'I have got myself into a state of holiness' (65:5) without any need for the Mosaic law, and so without the help of God. This people, then, who were adopting this 'holier-than-thou' attitude, were akin to the modern 'emancipated' person who sneers at the whole idea of revelation, and applies his or her new freedom to attack the Judaeo-Christian sexual ethic of the ages.

Paul D. Hanson (*The Dawn of Apocalyptic*) regards this 'holier-than-thou' group, not as the followers of Canaanite practices, but as those priests, sons of Zadok, who stand back from exercising *tsedaqah*, like the priest in Jesus' parable of the Good Samaritan (did Jesus take it from here?). Is it the case then that this party is so far from understanding the good news of God that they are as evil as those who practise the cults TI has just begun to describe? Is it they, then — the elite of Israel — who are 'a smoke in my nostrils'?

But the point to note is that prevenient grace still prevails. The exasperated Shepherd still regards the flock as his sheep. How difficult it is for self-opinionated people to realize the enor-

mity of their stance in despising the self-giving of God in his
almighty love. The word 'provoke' (*hik'is*) occurs some fifty times
in the OT to describe Israel's behaviour in angering God by
deserting him and going after other gods. Occurring as often as
it does, it seems to be telling us something about the constant
attitude of God in answer to their folly.

'Sacrificing in gardens' (cf. 57:5) refers to Canaanite 'high
places'. Such activities must have been carried on to false gods
and not at Yahweh's altar, which was then a mere primitive
structure, that 'the remnant of the people' (Hag. 1:14) had set
up amongst the rubble.

'Burning incense upon bricks' was an act belonging in some
false cult, the smell of which went up to God's 'face' as a deliberate provocation. Monotheists have but one choice and one only,
and must stick to that choice. The attractiveness of polytheism
is that it widens every choice and imposes no limitations upon
us human worshippers. Polytheism does not make demands upon
people.

Worship of the dead ('who sit in tombs') or ancestor worship
reveals a denial of grace, as does equally the concept of the transmigration of souls. For of course the dead are safe in God's care.
Our concern is to be for the living (Isa. 56:1-2).

Some of the community 'spend the night in secret places', that
is, practise incubation in order to learn what the future holds.
They do so by sleeping in vaults (8:19; 57:9), below ground level,
and so at the level of the grave. By this means they hope to learn
what the future holds through dreams granted them by the dead
in Sheol. The Dead Sea Isaiah scroll speaks here of a revolting
practice: 'They suck penises up to the testicles', with reference
it would seem to aberrant sexual practices in which Canaanites
indulged. The law of Moses pronounced such acts abhorrent
(Lev. 18:22).

The indication that they 'eat swine's flesh' shows that they
were ostentatiously rejecting the terms of the Covenant (Lev.
11:7; Deut. 14:8). The law of Moses forbade the eating of pork
that was employed by some Canaanites in the worship of 'un-
derground' divinities.

'Broth of abominable things' could mean eating rats and mice
(cf. Isa. 66:17). This was done, probably, not because of hunger
but in order to mix a 'hell's brew', like the witches in William

91

Shakespeare's *Macbeth*. [We note that the early Church condemned the eating of flesh that had been offered to idols (cf. Acts
15:29; 1 Cor. 8:1ff.), along with perverted sex, regarding these as
acts of rebellion against the reconstituted Covenant which had
been given it by Christ.]

In a word then, TI's fellow citizens had forgotten God's three-
fold 'requirement' of Israel that was meant to supplant all aberrant thoughts gained from the 'religions' of the world: justice,
love, and submission (Mic. 6:8). On the other hand, as Hanson
writes of Isa. 65:5: 'It is hardly an accident that this short sentence contains three of the cardinal technical terms in the priestly
language of the hierocratic tradition to express the special sanc-
tity of the Zadokite priesthood' (*The Dawn of Apocalyptic*, 147-48).

Church historians agree that the success of the Protestant Reformation in England brought new and terrible superstitions to
the surface amongst many illiterate folk. The traditional ritual
framework for dealing with daily misfortune and worry had been
destroyed, leaving many simple people more anxious than before;
so they turned to witchcraft and the occult, for no longer was
there an outlet in traditional sacramental magic and pilgrimage
piety. Norman Cohn suggests that this resort to the occult was
an unconscious resentment against Christianity as too strict a
religion, against Christ as too stern a taskmaster (*Europe's Inner
Demons*, 262). Steven Ozment declares that, 'the great shortcom-
ing of the Reformation was its naïve expectation that the majority
of people were capable of radical religious enlightenment and
moral transformation' (*The Age of Reform 1250 – 1550*, 437). This
is probably the situation we find here in the period before sacrificial worship was resumed in the rebuilt temple. It is a great
pity that the two parties which we find to be in opposition in these
chapters could not discover that neither emphasis can do without
the other. It is the two together that make a 'catholic' faith.

The Judgment of God (6-7)

God's Word ('it', here) is first uttered, and only then 'is written
before me'. Therefore we dare not brush aside its significance
(55:11). This imagery occurs also at Exod. 32:32-33; Dan. 7:10;
Mal. 3:16; Rev. 13:8. Our reference to Daniel even connects the
fire of God's wrath with 'the books' of judgment. So we are given
here a warning of what is to follow in the final chapter of this
long book of Isaiah.

God is a God of justice. Therefore he must necessarily punish the disloyal. We should note that God is not dealing here with his people as isolated individuals, a reality which many modern sects find it virtually impossible to grasp. The individualism of Californian sectist theology is based more upon Platonic philosophy than upon the Scriptures.

The pages of TI reveal to us the human search for the ultimate meaning of the idea of judgment. Some of the returnees saw the fall of Jerusalem in 587 B.C. as the moment of supreme judgment, the end spoken of by Amos (Amos 8:2). Others, as here (Isa. 65:6), see God's 'coming' as a continuing process. We find this reflected in the thought of the early Church, in its use of the Aramaic term *Maranatha* (e.g., 1 Cor. 16:22). For if the word is pronounced as *Maran-atha*, then it means 'The LORD has come'. If it is pronounced as *Marana-tha*, it means 'O LORD, come!' (cf. Isa. 26:16). So we can see with the help of TI that both usages are correct at the same time.

So God here speaks judgment with burning wrath. We recall that in his famous encyclical 'Mit brennender Sorge' ('With Burning Anxiety') Pope Pius XI in 1937 chose to use the language of this passage as he condemned the racism of the Nazi creed: 'I will not keep silent . . . because they burned incense upon the mountains'. The pope refuted the Nazi creed in terms of TI's theology:

> True Christianity proves itself in the love of God and the active love of one's neighbour. . . . He who wants to banish biblical history and the wisdom of the OT from school and church commits blasphemy against the Word of God.

'They burned incense . . .' marks a recrudescence and application of pagan myths to the life of a whole nation. God says here: 'I will repay (RSV 'measure') into their bosom' (that is, 'throw it back at them') 'their iniquities (or 'your', plural, in the Hebrew; see RSV mg) and their (again 'your' in Hebrew) fathers' iniquities together'. Is the child of a drunken father wholly and individually responsible if he or she goes to the bad? All through the OT the unit with which God deals first is the family; in the NT the whole story begins with the Holy Family. Modern Western people must be reminded that the four generations mentioned in the Second Commandment did not succeed each other in time.

93

Rather, all lived simultaneously in their village as one extended family, one pyschic unit (Exod. 20:10; cf. Acts 16:32; 1 Cor. 7:14). If this had not been the case, the concept of vicarious suffering (Isaiah 53) would never have seen the light of day.

God Himself Speaks Again (8-9)

This vicarious view of the interaction of personal relationships within the family of God (56:5-8) has a positive outcome as well as the negative one of the total responsibility that rests upon all Israel. It would seem that someone asked TI the question: What is Israel saved for? The concept of the remnant here is one that runs through all 'Isaiah' (1:9; 7:3; 10:20-22; 37:31; 46:3). So also is it the case with the metaphor of the vine, or of the vineyard (5:1-7). Here the two are placed together. Wine was always considered to be a blessing to mankind, even though an ambivalent one. At Ps. 104:15 we read that wine makes glad 'the heart of man'; but in Proverbs we find several warnings against its misuse (e.g., Prov. 20:1; 23:30-32). In the same way in the NT salt makes food edible, and people cannot do without it; but if too much is added to food, it makes them sick.

What connection has this metaphor then with 'Jacob'? Jacob was of course the 'father' of those northern tribes who were taken into exile as long ago as 721. 'Judah', on the other hand, was the 'father' of the south, where Jerusalem and Bethlehem lay. TI thus agrees with Ezekiel when the latter declared that God's remnant would come forth from amongst all the twelve tribes in exile (Ezek. 37:15-22). A blessing, we recall, is a word spoken, a declaration uttered with purpose and promise; it was full of potency. In the case of the imagery used here it fills the whole vine with vitality. The result of God's blessing of it therefore is that this remnant of Israel would in turn be a blessing to the world. Even the land which God has given to Israel is there only as a *pied-à-terre* (a temporary lodging) for Israel to use to this end. Of itself Israel is nothing. To revert to Jesus' parabolic picture, salt not used for making food edible demands judgment upon itself; it can only be used, as in snowbound cities today, to be stood on and crushed under foot. And so God's decision and judgment is of grace alone, and is made in accordance with the *hesed* which is the essence of his Covenant made with Israel.

We note that God lays down no conditions, such as that Israel should first repent. All he says is that 'my chosen shall inherit it'—not in order that Israel might be saved while other nations are damned, but that the world, through the chosen Servant, might be saved (Isa. 43:12; 49:6). Those who seek today to look for an 'interfaith theology', or 'a theology for the future', and such like should keep TI's divine speech firmly in mind.

10-12 'Sharon' in those days was a swamp, not a fit place for domestic animals. When later on it was reclaimed it became proverbially very fertile (33:9; 35:2). 'The Valley of Achor' too was proverbially accursed because it was a barren gorge. 'Achor' derives from a verb meaning 'to break a taboo'. At Josh. 7:26 it is rendered by 'trouble' (RSV mg) through punning, with the idea that Achan 'broke the taboo' that God had laid upon Israel. Hosea employed that incident to point to the manner in which God can take even what is accursed—in fact, the worst thing an Israelite could do was to break God's Covenant of Grace—and turn even that into 'a door of hope' (Hos. 2:15). TI remembers also the words of Ezekiel: 'I will bring you into the wilderness of the peoples, and there will I enter into judgment with you face to face' (Ezek. 20:35). God had to do so again and again as Israel succumbed to the forces of evil and chaos—even of a cross, as we might add. God is the one who not merely creates; he may actually create good out of evil, out of chaos (Gen. 1:2-3).

As for those who, like Achan, break faith with God, who give their loyalty to the Syrian gods 'Fortune' and 'Destiny', these must face the judgment of God. The believing psalmist had said, 'Thou preparest a table before me' (Ps. 23:5). Here humankind prepares a gambling table, not before God, but before the goddess of luck. Then, in a strong wordplay upon the name Destiny (*meni*; cf. Dan. 5:25), we read, 'I will destine (meni) you to the sword'. If worship of this deity did actually persist for another thousand years, then she is mentioned again in the Koran at Sura 53:20.

TI has mentioned the fascinating power gambling has upon a person, such as to make him a slave to its insidious nature (Isa. 65:11). So now in v. 12 he has God say, 'You chose what I did not delight in', choosing of your own free will to be a slave. Thus vv. 13-16 describe the effects of the blessing and the curse enunciated so long before (cf. Deut. 30:15-20).

95

Promise and Threat (13-16)

Eating, drinking, and rejoicing are all elements in God's invitation at 55:1-2. But now, what we hear four times in succession is 'Behold, my servants shall . . . but you shall. . . .' The last of the four is 'But you shall scream from hearts in despair (author's translation), and shall wail for anguish of spirit' (cf. Matt. 8:12). Disloyalty is Israel's basic sin. But loyalty is the mark of God's faithfulness, his *hesed*, his 'steadfast love'. Disloyalty therefore can lead only to 'hell'. It is only the one who 'shall bless himself by the God of truth' who will be known by the new name, the New Israel, for such alone are 'his servants'. The word 'truth' means that God is trustworthy, faithful, the God one can be sure of, the God who will never let you go. Not only so, he is the 'all-knowing God who forgets' (!): 'the former troubles are forgotten and are hid from my eyes'. This is such a shocking statement to come out of the mouth of God that the LXX refuses to translate it. All that version has is 'It shall not come into their mind'. Unfortunately, the pre-Reformation Church did not use the Hebrew text of our Bible, and had to rely upon the LXX for its knowledge of the book of Isaiah.

The New Creation (17-19)

The creeds of the Church were drawn up in the early Christian centuries within a world view very different from that of the OT prophets. So the creeds begin: 'I believe in one God the Father Almighty, *Maker* of heaven and earth. . . .' Only secondly thereafter comes the confession that God is also the Redeemer, and only after the name of Jesus Christ has been mentioned! For TI, however, creation is what comes forth out of God's redeeming love. The prophet's understanding of Torah was that God had made himself known first as the Redeemer, at that point in history when he rescued Israel out of Egypt in the days of Moses. Yet now, he declares, God has once again revealed himself in a redemptive action when he brought home to Jerusalem the very generation of Israelites whom TI is even now addressing. What is more, that act of God is also a creative act. He had now created the *New* Israel by means of his 'creative' love and self-emptying. Thus since he had now done so twice, there was no need to suppose that he would not make a habit of it! Consequently, what

we now hear is: '(Realize) that (*ki*) I am creating new heavens
and a new earth' (God himself is speaking). The word 'create'
here could be a future form of the verb. But what we are to
recognize is that God's creative activity is really a continuation,
an outflow, from Gen. 1:1: 'When God began to create the heavens and the earth' (RSV mg). So this active participle shows
that God is not required to make a repair job on a world that is
in a mess.

God is not a *deus ex machina* such as the Greek tragedians
employed to right the wrongs of their city and people in one great
magical act. God is continually bringing good out of evil, life out
of death. Martin Luther declared that the constant re-creation
of sinful human beings showed more than anything else that the
creator God is essentially nothing other than the outpouring of
love. Incidentally, moreover, TI is warning us here (if we might
use him today for evidence) that the first chapter of Genesis is
not a scientific document over which 'creationists' and 'evolu-
tionists' can continue to argue, but is an expression of God's
loving purpose and plan for the universe he has created for the
good of mankind.

As before, the LXX, written in the atmosphere of Platonic
philosophy, translates here only by 'There shall be a new heaven.
. . .' Thus it shows that its authors had not grasped the significance of the verb *bara* (cf. Isa. 51:6), which describes an *act* of
creative love and purpose. In fact, since God is always re-creat-
ing, bringing new life out of death, then the concept of 'the end'
becomes a technical term to denote distinct, different points of
the eschatological timetable, or no specific point, or more than
one point (M. E. Stone, 'Coherence and Inconsistency in the
Apocalypses: The Case of "the End" in 4 Ezra', *JBL* 102 [1983]:
238). TI thus understands the purposes of God quite differently
from the millenarian or adventist views of some present-day sections of the Church.

Yet again, TI's insight offers us the clue we need to understand
what both Testaments mean by miracle. We are to remember
that the word 'supernatural', although apparently coined by
Pseudo-Dionysius (ca. A.D. 500), was made an accepted theological term by Thomas Aquinas in the 13th century. 'Supernatural' is not a biblical word. However, following Thomas' use of
this Aristotelian mode of thinking, the biblical miracles came to

be understood as an invasion of the natural by the supernatural. The biblical witnesses, on the other hand, are involved in the totality of the world. They regard miracles rather as a new and surprising mode of God's ongoing activity. Paul Tillich puts it thus:

> Providence is not interference; it is creation. It uses all factors, both those given by freedom and those given by destiny, in creatively directing everything towards its fulfilment. . . . It is not an additional factor, a miraculous physical or mental interference in terms of supranaturalism [his term]. (*Systematic Theology* 1:267)

Thus what follows is not to be described as being 'apocalyptic in embryo', though we may see it as being just on the edge of it. Rather, it speaks of the ultimate meaning of God's re-creative love at each moment that he 'visits' his people, or even each individual person. On the other hand, it may at the same time be speaking of the endpoint of his redemptive purpose, the eschaton. Thus the word *bara* is 'eschatological' in content, and the passage here is more 'eschatological' than 'apocalyptic' in nature. The endpoint to which it refers is seen as the final forgiveness of God of all that is past. So absolute is this new act of his (of which the 'Return' is but the firstfruits), that 'the former things shall not be remembered or come into mind' (as at Jer. 3:16). This ultimate act of God will be like when the light shines in the darkness but cannot be overcome. From our human angle, of course, the vision given us in the following passage can be grasped only when we think of it as a vision of the future. But TI thinks of it as eternally present, in that the present is what determines eternity (cf. Jesus' teaching at Matt. 25:31-46). Yet the link our thinking seeks, when it tries to understand this difficult issue, is not to be expressed in these worldly terms. Rather, it is to be found in the nature of God, in that he is the God who forgives and who, in forgiving, renews.

The eschatological significance of the ruins of the decadent city of Jerusalem in the prophet's day is therefore no less than 'rejoicing' and the people of the city 'joy'. Life lived in the faith of God's re-creative love is one of joy. This is why some theologians have named the OT 'The Book of Joy'. They have done so because God himself is joy — joy in knowing that Israel is

forgiven and that they are now the New Israel, by grace alone.
God himself says (v. 19) 'I will rejoice *in* Jerusalem, and be glad
in my people'. Once again, unfortunately, the LXX has not
grasped the wonder of such a profound utterance. It says only
'They shall find in her joy and exultation'.

So then, God himself is joy. We read that God commands us
to maintain this eschatological joy now, although being eschatological it belongs to him: 'Be glad in that which I create; for
. . . *I* will rejoice in Jerusalem'. Accordingly, if this is how God
feels about his people, then we his people are meant to do so
also, that is, experience joy in the people who are our neighbours.
Once again the LXX neglects to see this vision in terms of grace,
for it translates *bara* ('create') by *poio* ('I make'). But we must
also observe that the vision requires both matter and spirit to
become actual. It requires earth as well as heaven or, as we might
say, things as well as persons. For 'the land', or 'earth', or 'matter' is always necessary for God's saving purposes, a concept in
tune with the two moments in the life of Christ that we call the
beginning and the end. In the NT we read that the Word became
'flesh', and that the Resurrection is to be understood in terms of
'matter'.

Eschatology (20-25)

This strophe offers us a case of 'realized eschatology'. It gives a
picture of what God is actually creating now, and which arises,
and goes on arising out of all our 'nows'. We can understand this
term best by employing our modern terms 'sacrament' and 'sacramental' to explain it. The idea of a child living to be 'a hundred
years old' pictures the totally fulfilled life, one without tragedy
or pain, in the same sense as John 10:10. It tells us that life here
and now has potentially total meaning. That is one side of the
coin, the side we can see with our eyes. Its other side, however,
is what we cannot see; that is the totally fulfilled life in eternity,
yet an eternity that is not to be conceived as timeless. For if it
were so, then we would be denied all hope of growth in joy and
love beyond death.

The phrase 'they shall plant vineyards and eat their fruit'
describes the joy of a fulfilled vocation, of seeing the fruits of
one's labours (cf. 53:11), of discovering that ordinary daily life
has ultimate significance. Again, 'the eternal gift of the land' is

also needed in this sacramental picture. For it shows that God is offering here and now, not the immortality of the soul (a Greek and Hindu concept), but a life knowing full satisfaction. God offers life lived in all the fulness of his grace, a life that is nourished by prayer and by fellowship with God at all times (65:24), and increasingly so in eternity. Gone then is the old concept of Sheol of the earlier books of the OT (cf. 38:10), where death without God was a descent into shadowy nothingness. Gone is the despair of the world about the meaninglessness of the fact that countless babies die annually almost at birth, or even before birth takes place. The centenarian who, despite his physical strength, has 'missed out' (*hata*) on fellowship with God in the here and now, will know in eternity the meaning of being cursed, of 'missing out' on eternal life (Deut. 30:1, 19; Rev. 22:3). A child will not be born 'for sudden terror' (*labbehalah* RSV mg), as for an unexpected crib death or to be the victim of flood or radioactive fallout. This is because children too belong in Yahweh's Covenant of Grace. The Garden of Eden has been restored, and the tensions of society no longer exist. This perfection has not been reached through meditation but through the structures of history, for time and place have not been obliterated.

Here we find no trace of what the secularist today calls 'pie in the sky', of a heaven to which individual souls are transmitted as they are plucked out of an evil world or released from the weight of their human bodies. The biblical heaven is social, where all are in fellowship both with God and with one another, and a heaven where matter matters! As TI so clearly shows, it is sin that separates between God and mankind and between one person and another. It is not body, not space and time. In consequence, entrance to this heaven that TI looks for comes about only through an act of God. That act is his act of forgiveness. 'Before they call I will answer', for God's grace is prevenient grace. 'The lion shall eat straw like the ox', for the 'world' too will have been redeemed, and not merely the souls of people. And so the two-sided dream of Isaiah will have been realized when all nations will flow up to the house of the LORD, to be found on the highest of the mountains (Isa. 2:1-5), and 'the earth shall be full of the knowledge of the LORD as the waters cover the sea' (11:9).

CHAPTER 66

HEAVEN AND HELL
Isaiah 66:1-24

Where Is God To Be Found?

More than one person seems to be responsible for this chapter. It appears to be a collection of snippets from sermons, vv. 1-6 being the longest amongst them. However, some of the utterances here, unlike virtually all that has gone before, are written in prose and not in verse.

Then again, to what date should we ascribe this collection? Nowhere in this third section of Isaiah is there any mention made of Sheshbazzar, the political head of state appointed by King Cyrus. There is no reference either to Haggai or Zechariah (whose books appear in the OT), both of whom come to the fore about 520 B.C. Nor has any mention been made till now of the temple, apart from references to what must have been open-air worship round a partly-built altar. At Hag. 1:9 we learn that God's 'house' was still in ruins. So we see a party arising, calling themselves 'the remnant of the people' (see Isa. 10:20, where this title is given to the 'survivors'). The moving spirits of this new party seem to have been the prophet Haggai and Zerubbabel, the grandson of Jehoiachin (2 Kgs. 24:8-17) and thus of the Davidic line, who was the appointee of the Persian government as governor of Judah. And with Zerubbabel we associate the name of Joshua, the high priest, whom we have not met before either. These all had returned from Babylon at an unknown date or dates. We should note then that it was not 'the people of the land' who urged the rebuilding of the temple, but returnees from the Exile (Ezra 6:16, 19).

Over against this group, again, the 'evangelic' group represented by TI seemed to feel no more need for a temple than did the Qumran community in the century before Christ. They seemed

to accept the idea that God's need of a holy 'place' had ended
with the fall of Jerusalem, so that instead of such a building the
concept of a holy 'time' had grown up. This was aided, it would
seem, by TI's emphasis upon the sabbath; and this in turn was
leading to the concept of continual re-creation (Isa. 66:1). Moreover, this particular emphasis continues on into rabbinical Judaism, for which the word *'olam* means both created space and
eternity of time.

Haggai is called 'the messenger of the LORD' (Hag. 1:13). In
Hebrew this word could be written as *Malachi* ('my messenger').
Zechariah, in his turn, referred to God's express Word as addressing the high priest in the form of 'the angel of the LORD'
(the same word as 'messenger' above; Zech. 3:6), thereby giving
him authority to 'rule my house and have charge of my courts'
(v. 7) once the temple should be rebuilt. But at the same time
Zechariah seems to have regarded Zerubbabel as the contemporary messianic figure, son of David, and so as the 'Branch' of
which both Isaiah and Jeremiah had spoken (Isa. 11:1; Jer. 23:5;
33:15). Isaiah 66, coming as it does at the end of our collection
of interpretative prophecy, or theological thought, seems thus to
contain the theology of at least three different parties amongst
the inhabitants of Jerusalem. A unifying factor, however, is that
the two prophetic hopes of Ezekiel, that of the 'resurrection' of
Israel and that of the rebuilding of the temple, are prefaced
equally by the phrase 'the hand of the LORD was upon me' (Ezek.
37:1; 40:1).

We are to remember that Ezekiel had seen the glory depart
from the ruins of the temple (10:18-19) yet believed that it had
removed only to Babylon, where it rested over the dejected exiles.
But he had also believed that the glory would return to Jerusalem
once God had brought his people home and once the temple was
rebuilt and dedicated (48:35). At this point in history, however,
the temple had not yet been begun. It would seem that the
prophet whose words we have in Isa. 66:1-2 does not believe that
it is God's will that the temple should be rebuilt. For him the
locus of the sacred is no longer such a building but is rather
human possibility, humanity's future, mankind's destiny, broken
indeed by sin yet restorable and transformable by God. That
must include the humanization of mankind and the transformation of society. This will eventuate only if people humble

themselves before God, let God destroy their ego, and permit
God Almighty ('all these things are mine') to perfect his will with
humankind.

The uninitiated can be perplexed if they are told that the NT
contains no one specific doctrine of atonement. In the same way,
this long book of Isaiah likewise finishes up with at least three
views of what God had planned for Israel's future, now that his
tsedeq had become a fact of history.

1-2 This is evidently not the same voice that gave us ch. 65. He
begins by speaking as from God and using virtually the same
words that Nathan had used to King David at 2 Sam. 7:5b. He
begins not with 'Thus says the LORD' (RSV) but with 'Thus the
LORD *has said*', on the ground that what he has said is the application of what is to be found in the *torah* now being applied
to the contemporary moment. Then he speaks as if heaven and
earth were one. This concept may be based on TI's good Hebraic
monistic view, as against the dualistic thought of Greece and the
Orient where heaven and earth are opposites. In God's sight they
are one. This means that God can be worshipped equally as
Transcendent Being and as Immanent Friend. Because of this
there is no need for a special 'house' where God is to be found,
such as a temple; for 'the place of my rest' cannot be confined
to a building made by human hands.

A group of Israelites had newly settled, not in Babylon, but
in Egypt. There at Elephantine, a Jewish military colony near
Aswan, they had built a temple to Yahweh. But soon their worship became corrupted through the influence of the ideologies of
the Egyptians. Yahweh was even given a wife, who was known
as the Queen of Heaven (Jer. 44:15-19). We note how later on,
when the Samaritans established a temple for themselves on Mt.
Gerizim, their religion became completely introspective and finally faded out.

What this voice is saying is that, since the eschaton has begun,
Zion itself is sufficient as the firstfruits of the heavenly temple.
In other words, this speaker is aware that the New Israel is now
living in what modern German theologians have called the *Zwi-
schenzeit*, the 'time in between'.

That God had chosen Jerusalem was a belief basic to the
particularism of the biblical faith. That God had called for one

103

particular 'house' for his worship goes back to his particularistic choice of David and of David's son, so that Solomon's temple could be known even as God's 'footstool' (Ps. 99:5; Lam. 2:1; see 2 Sam. 7:1-6; 1 Kgs. 5:5; 8:12-13; Ps. 11:4; 132:7-8). Yet in the NT we hear Stephen, before his martyrdom, quoting our present passage (Acts 7:47-50) to suggest that Solomon had been mistaken to tie God down in this way.

Yet the question arises: as the large, excited group of priests, Levites, and temple servants now present in Jerusalem (Ezra 2:36-54) — having been aroused from their lethargy and lack of faith by Haggai — were arguing and discussing and planning to rebuild the temple, was what they were doing in contradiction to the thought of the first voice? In the light of Isa. 65:17, was a temple of any kind not one of those valuable elements in the past of Israel's faith out of which God was now creating something new? Would it then be 'new' in the sense that the temple of old 'shall not be remembered or come into mind' (Isa. 65:17; cf. Rev. 21:22)? In other words, was this first voice in fact inviting his priestly brethren to think eschatologically, rather than in terms of space and time, bricks and mortar? There have always been groups from amongst both Jews and Christians who have tended to disregard the present as being unimportant in comparison with the heavenly vision.

But then the heavenly vision is not just something laid up for the future. It is also to be found in 'the man to whom I will look, he that is humble and contrite in spirit' (literally, 'broken and needing repairing'). In fact, the group described here that 'trembles at my word' has even been dubbed with the (anachronistic!) name of Quakers! (see 66:5). By the word 'contrite' (*'ani*) we understand a wounded heart, humbling the individual to the earth so that he is not able to rise (see 49:13; cf. Luke 6:20-22, along with the Magnificat, 1:46-55). If we are not in such a condition, then we must be prepared to be humbled by the mighty hand of God to our shame and disgrace, as John Calvin comments here. What God looks for is obedience, not ritual, not ecstatic worship, but a personal acceptance of God's call to be his suffering servant. This experience can be heard and known directly by an individual man or woman without the aid of a temple or of any human activity.

The first voice is thus handling an important issue. It is that God addresses us by his Word. The Chinese word for love means

something quite different from the Swahili word that we so translate, because in each case the concept behind the word is rooted
in two different cultures. Human beings with their very different
cultures discover that none of them can interpret the content of
the Word of God (Isa. 55:8-9). All that man can do, says this
voice, is to 'tremble at his word'.

3-4 Perhaps then we are to take the middle way between what
the first voice seems to be saying and what a second voice main-
tains in the following two verses. Here the author goes on to
extraordinarily literalistic extremes to denounce the whole sacrificial cult that may be associated with any temple. But Isaiah
of Jerusalem seems to have done so already (Isa. 1:10-17). 'He
who (ritualistically) slaughters an ox (for sacrifice)' is only one
half of a sentence. The other half runs: 'him who "smites" ('kills',
as RSV?) a man'. Is the RSV in order when it places the word
'like' between the two statements, though it is not there in the
original? Does this voice mean to say 'He who sacrifices an ox
in the worship of Yahweh is as bad as a murderer'? Or again, is
the innocent act of handling a 'cereal offering' as wrong as offering 'swine's blood', for of course handling pigs is taboo? In the
light of 1:12-17, however, is not what he is wanting to say just
this, that such practices must not be continued by the self-righteous, whose heart is far from God? If so, then is he not merely
repeating the words of 65:12? For there they 'chose their own
way in which I did not delight' (author's translation). So God
will in return 'choose affliction for them', he says (66:4). Again,
sacrificing a lamb was an ancient institution and clearly goes
back to the command of God (Exod. 12:21); yet the voice says
it is really no different from breaking 'a dog's neck'. Perhaps this
is the exaggerated Semitic way of likening the Zadokite priests
once again to those who commit 'abominations'. We may suppose
so, since the 'also' with which Isa. 66:4 begins (*gam*) is a particle
used before a solemn statement. Here then it opens an expression
of the divine wrath, such as we have already heard at 65:12, and
with which we are to meet again and again throughout the whole
Bible (e.g., Ps. 52:5; Ezek. 16:43; Mal. 2:9; Matt. 11:21-24).

5 A third voice, though only a short interjection, makes a very
weighty statement. The speaker declares that it is not his words,

but 'the word of the LORD' that he is uttering. Perhaps this individual is seeking to mediate between the various parties. He turns to those for whom the first voice speaks and declares: 'Please be reasonable. God says, "There are those who actually hate you and cast you out for my name's sake" ' (author's translation). The words 'cast out' are very emphatic. They form a pun upon the word 'menstruation', a natural process which was considered to render a woman unclean (Lev. 12:5). The verb is found with this double meaning again at Amos 6:3. We can see how, therefore, in later Hebrew it came to mean 'excommunicate'. But, the voice goes on, there are also those who believe we should build the temple to the glory of God, and who thus desire to 'let the LORD be glorified'. The tables will then be turned. 'We' shall 'see your joy', but 'they' in turn 'shall be put to shame'. So perhaps the speaker was one of the disenfranchised Levites. He would know his Torah well, and so could declare on its basis 'Hear the word of the LORD'. They were opposed by the pragmatic, realistic Zadokites who were also pressing for a rebuilt temple, but on their terms. How broadminded then TI was to include these opposing views in his 'book'.

Strong terms such as these may represent the very terse Hebrew of this verse; yet it would be wrong to suggest the above to be the only meaning of these lines. Anyway, they are an instance of the vigorous and even crude form of ancient Semitic speech, such as we find frequently in Ezekiel (e.g., Ezek. 9:7; 16:15-43; cf. Jesus' virtual quotation from 13:10-11 at Matt. 23:27) and later on in much of Martin Luther's writings.

However, this verse may be — and in fact is — construed differently by other editors. 'Your brethren who hate you' may refer to the descendants of those Israelites who had never been in Babylon, and who were now known as the *'am ha-arets,* the 'people of the land'. They had long ago taken possession of the properties that had belonged to the exiles of old. Now the rightful owners had returned and were very naturally claiming these properties as their own. In consequence, antagonism and jealousy had developed between the two parties. A good illustration of this situation occurred in 1945 when Hungarian Jews, survivors (cf. Isa. 45:20) of the Nazi concentration and forced-labour camps, returned home to Budapest. They came back, not as living skeletons, but as well-fed and well-clothed protegees of the Allies, naturally expecting to repossess their shops and businesses, which they were entitled to do by law. But of course those non-Jews who had expropriated these businesses 'hated' the returnees for claiming their rights.

6 A fourth voice requires only one verse to make his point. He upholds the party that plans to rebuild the temple. From his standpoint, therefore, he declares that God will roar from the temple his righteous judgment upon 'his enemies'. Who these enemies are we are not told. But then Isaian theology recognizes that all people are God's enemies. This 'voice' may have taken his language from Amos 1:2 or Joel 3:16. The content of his single short utterance is poetic and awesome; but, along with Isa. 33:14, it offers a good introduction to elements in the eschatological passage to follow at 66:15-16. The temple (or perhaps the altar being used at the moment) was where people spoke to God in prayer. 'The voice of the LORD' was thus in answer to the voice of Israel.

Extract from a Sermon (7-11)

The outstanding issue in this sermon is the principle, explained by means of several illustrations, of how God works towards his end of creating a new heaven and a new earth. Isaiah had rebuked those who informed God that he should 'make haste . . . let the purpose of the Holy One of Israel draw near, and let it come, that we may know it' (Isa. 5:19). He had done so because he was aware that people's ideas about God's plans are bound to be wrong, even, in fact, evil. So here TI takes up the issue by showing that God will execute his plan in his own good time, not in ours; yet the moment of its execution will definitely come (66:9), because God has promised that it will.

Central here is that God is Creator. God creates his kingdom by bringing something new out of the old, just as at the beginning he brought light out of chaos. He acts in this way effortlessly and quietly, and may do so 'in one day'. He may act so decisively that 'the former troubles are forgotten', and are even 'hid from God's eyes' (65:16).

The first illustration is that of childbirth. With God working in and through this natural function the 'new' baby emerges quietly without labour pains from the (old) body of its mother.

There it is — suddenly, unexpectedly present when no one imagined such a birth was due. While at Exod. 4:22 God had told Moses 'Israel is my first-born son', we are to remember that God's people are spoken of also as 'she', in fact as the virgin, or as the virgin daughter. In various forms we find this usage appearing at Isa. 37:22; Jer. 18:13; 31:4, 21; Lam. 1:15; 2:13; Amos 5:2. (See G. A. F. Knight, 'The Protestant World and Mariology', *SJT* 19 [1966]: 55-73.)

We would suggest that the intention of this sermon was twofold. First, we are meant to move from the illustration of the birth of any baby to a particular boy baby, a son who would be 'new'. Second, we are to move from the illustration of Israel as mother to that of Mother Jerusalem (Isa. 66:10-11; cf. 60:1, where Israel is spoken of in the feminine).

The birth of a baby is an astonishing thing; it is a miracle wrought by the Creator. 'Rejoice with Jerusalem', they cry. 'It's a boy!' The verb 'delivered' means actually 'allowed to escape' (*himlitah*). At 3:15 this same verb is used of God's 'letting escape from the womb' the remnant of which Isaiah has so much to say. The historical fact facing the returnees, then, was that God's holy Spirit had in fact come upon their virgin mother, Zion (61:1). Thus the pains of the Exile which Israel had endured were actually the pains of labour. Now that Mother Israel is back home from Babylon, she will therefore bring forth a new generation of the People of God, to be known as the New Israel. You returnees, he says, are to rejoice that you and your generation have been 'born again' from Zion, your virgin mother. 'Rejoice in (not 'for') Jerusalem' (cf. 65:19). Don't mourn over her (cf. 61:3) in the sense that some people declare pessimistically today 'The Church is dead'. For the keynote of the new life in the New Jerusalem is to be joy. What happened under Cyrus in the year 538 is to be seen as an eschatological moment, a sacramental sign of something greater still to come. God has by no means 'shut the womb' and so ceased to create (see 66:22). Indeed, he is still 'your God' (v. 9b). 'You may drink deeply (literally 'quaff') with delight from the abundance of her glory.' Zion has no glory of herself, of course; her glory is wholly the gift of God's grace and loving purpose for her and her numerous progeny.

TI is here speaking from his heart, for he now possesses the immense satisfaction of knowing who he is and what he exists

for. Clearly he is now utterly aware that God is his Father, that
Zion is his Mother, and that he is a child of the union between
them. As Karl Barth puts it, it is through this revealed order that
an individual may find a personal faith (*Dogmatics*, 4/1-3; cf. Isa.
62:5; Gal. 4:26). Moreover, because one has discovered himself
to be a child of the Covenant he need not seek farther for a
meaning to his life. For since the purpose and even the very being
of God is mission, and since the purpose of the New Israel is to
be mission, so 'as one whom his mother comforts' (Isa. 66:13)
Israel too has found its life's purpose. That purpose is to do the
will of the Father in love and in mission to all mankind, now that
the son knows the joy and peace of forgiveness within his own
heart.

Let us note then, that all this is a Word from God. It is not
a mere recommendation; it is a divine command. The New Land
(v. 8) is, of course, the Old Land of Palestine. But it too is 're-
created' when the Creator creates (*bara*) it as the firstfruits of the
new heaven and the new earth (see Jer. 31:1-6). At Isa. 66:9 the
RSV rendering does not bring out this emphasis in full. Rather,
the verse should be rendered: 'As for Me, shall I . . . shall I
. . . Yahweh keeps on saying'. For we are hearing God revealing
to us the eternal reality that he is always working, always creating, now and eternally.

12-14   This excerpt supplements and enlarges upon the eschatological picture above. At 48:18 we read how Israel while still
in exile had not yet received the gift of God's *shalom*. For one
thing they had not yet learned to obey their LORD. But now,
God's *tsedeq* had changed all that. Through grace Jerusalem was
now to receive 'prosperity' (*shalom*, 'peace'), the word that the
OT uses to describe the physical, moral, mental, psychical, and
spiritual wholeness which is that perfection and fulness of life
which Yahweh has in store in love for his people. This is not, of
course, the same as that perfect society which a philosophy such
as Marxism works for, a manmade heaven on earth. The latter
could only be pursued by sinful mankind. This is a God-given
creation, which will emerge from the old even as a child emerges
from the womb.

Thus the picture language of this passage is not to be taken
literally, but rather as poetry based upon the very different con-

ceptions of space and time held by the world in TI's day. It is
not good enough for us therefore merely to repeat the poetry we
read here, for example as the OT lesson in church, without com-
ment in this new age of science. We are obliged to use all the
scientific and theological data available to us to think through
and apply the significance of these poetic pictures of the truth of
God's promises to the nature of the strange new world we live in
today.

'A river' (*nahar*), such as the Nile, overflows annually over
what would otherwise be desert land. But it brings that land to
life, so that people can grow food on it for themselves. Such a
river is well pictured for us in Ezek. 47:1-12.

'A stream' (*nahal*) is a Near Eastern wadi. For much of the
year a wadi is a dry riverbed. But when the rains come it is 'an
overflowing stream'. Thus when 'the nations' bring their 'wealth'
to Zion, they will be overflowingly generous in their gratitude to
God that he has spoken, even to them — unworthy Gentiles as
they are — the promise of his great *shalom*.

The picture of a child carried on its mother's 'hip' is an extension of Isa. 66:11. By means of this imagery the kindliness,
love, and care of Mother Zion is emphasised. And if we have a
reference here also to 49:22 and 60:4, then it tells us that those
Israelites who are still living in dispersion will be welcomed home
to what one interpreter understands as 'Zion's ample bosom'.
But the Gentiles also will accompany the dispersed People of
God home to Zion. And so the word goes out to all the earth:
'As one whom his mother comforts, so I will comfort you'. The
day of 'comfort' (*naham*), the word used at 40:1 ('Comfort, comfort my people', in the sense of 'be comforted'), is what Luke
2:25 calls 'the consolation of Israel'.

In a word then, what we have here is a picture of idyllic peace,
of happy, healthy children no longer in danger of a serpent's bite,
but now being 'dandled upon' their mother's 'knees' (cf. Isa.
11:8). But this is what Israel actually is in God's sight, a child
(Hos. 11:1-4), and what Jesus expects the New Israel to be, children in their faith (John 13:3). Again, the trusting parent-child
relationship seen here is a picture of complete freedom, freedom
from anxiety about oneself. It speaks of composure, or freedom
from all purely human rules and regulations, whether political,
ecclesiastical, or moral. Absolute trust has thus engendered *hesed*

(Isa. 54:8; 63:7) in the beloved child, loyal steadfast love in place of coercion, such as reveals a total awareness of forgiveness and acceptance.

On the other hand, since we are handling an eschatological picture, what we are seeing is 'the other side of the coin' that has to do with the nature, not of Mother Zion, but of the God of eternity himself. Thus the passage also reveals to us the 'mother love' of the living God, for Zion is called to do and to be on earth what God is like in his eternity.

Because *shalom* covers also physical health and well-being (cf. Job 21:24, 'your bones will retain the freshness of youth and be full of sap' author's translation), they shall be able to 'see' that the joy in their hearts is from God, and to 'know', in an existential sense, that 'the hand of the LORD is with his servants'. ('Hand' represents the idea of strength and power; see also Luke 1:35, 51.) But 'his indignation is against his enemies'.

15-16 These two verses are sufficient to interpret the last phrase of v. 14 by means of a theophany of judgment, built with a marvellous minimum of words from such passages as 13:3-16; 29:6; 30:27-28; 34:1-17. This seeming contradiction between *shalom* as God's plan and his 'judgment' is dealt with later on in this chapter. We are not to forget that God's answer to the fact of human sin is that his life-giving waters can actually become 'waters of contradiction' (Num. 20:13; cf. Luke 12:51).

Much biblical theology is enshrined in the imagery of fire that follows. 'Fire' can incorporate within itself the paradox of destruction and of the cleansing which Isaiah had looked for at 1:21-26. It would be folly to judge the following passage by what *we* think 'fire' means here. Rather, we must seek to discover what it meant to TI.

First, fire is representative of the nature of God himself, as Deut. 4:24 declares: 'The LORD your God is a devouring fire'. Verse 33 reveals an astonishing relationship between God and Israel: 'Did any people ever hear the voice of a god speaking out of the midst of the fire, as you have heard, and still live?' We are to remember that this verse forms part of the 'quintessence of OT faith' (as some OT theologians suggest) that belongs in the core of passages comprising Deut. 4:32-34; 6:4-9, 20-25; 26:5-19; Josh. 24:1-28. As Deut. 6:7 insists: 'You shall teach them dili-

111

gently to your children'. These passages thus certainly formed the central 'creed' of the returned exiles. The verbs in this collection all occur in the past tense, for they have been uttered once and for all; thus they belong, not only to the here-and-now, but also to the eternity of God's purposes. Because this is so, centuries after the period of Moses Deuteronomy could come to be written. Furthermore, DI could also make the statement from within the Exile, 'When you walk through fire you shall not be burned', because God is there with you in the fire (Isa. 43:2); in fact, he is the fire. This deep conception was later explained (after TI's day) in the form of a midrash, a picture-parable for the ordinary person to grasp, in the story of the burning fiery furnace. In it we see that to be cast therein was to be cast upon God (Dan. 3:13-30). Ironically, in this story the king asks, 'Who is the god that will deliver you out of my hands?' (v. 15). The postbiblical Apocalypse of Abraham pursues the theme throughout Abraham's life, recalling that he came from the city named Ur, which in Hebrew means both 'light' and 'flame of fire' (Isa. 50:11). It is followed by *Genesis Rabbah* xxxviii.19 (on Gen. 11:28) and in Jubilees 12:12-24. Yet even as we ponder the interpretation given us of God's nature in those books, we are to recall TI's insistence that God is still 'stooping' (Isa. 63:9) even as he marches forth as fire, and that the Warrior is also the Servant, so that it is his blood which he pours forth *in* his beloved people.

Second, fire is representative of judgment, of the judgment of the God of wrath (see *TDNT* 5: 392, 399). This concept is made graphic when we read that God's wrath is 'kindled', or that fire burned in his nose (as at Isa. 65:5). For this understanding of fire, see 9:5; 10:16-17; 30:27; Ps. 68:2; 78:21; 79:5.

Third, when God 'sends' his fires of judgment (here we put together the preceding two interpretations) he sends himself, so to speak. The day is long gone when theologians spoke of the 'attributes' of God, as if these were commodities that we could detach from God and examine as objects in themselves. Thus when God sends fire upon a city wall (Amos 1:4, 7, 10, 12, 14), it means that he comes in person in judgment and in wrath as the God of Fire. It remains to be said that NT theology merely continues this theme (e.g., Matt. 3:11; Acts 2:3).

Fire can thus be a figure for war, war that God himself sends.

But then his is a war, not just against Gaza and Tyre, but against the powers of evil in both heaven and earth.

At Isa. 30:27; 33:14 God's fire is equated with his name, the representation of his very self. From that mode of speaking the whole realm of God's glory, the outer manifestation of his essential being — the 'apparel' of God made visible to the human eye — is also patently conceivable in terms of fire (Exod. 24:17; Joel 2:30; repeated in the NT at Acts 2:19). At Ps. 104:4 the angels (the word means 'sent forth') are shooting flames which perform the will of the fire from which they issue. Fire and tempest were thus the usual accompaniments of a divine theophany, when God unveiled his self (Isa. 29:6; 30:27; cf. Ps. 50:3) or sent forth his Word (Deut. 5:22) or when he entered into judgment with the forces of evil (Ezek. 38:22).

The fires of God, however, cannot be merely capricious flames, sent against the powers of evil in his anger and wrath (Ps. 89:46). God is the Holy God, and so the fire of his wrath is his holy fire. Isaiah had declared that this 'Holy One' (Isa. 10:17) 'shows himself holy in righteousness' (5:16b). We have seen from ch. 56 what that latter verse means for the whole of 'Isaiah'.

Since God's fire is the profound and ultimate picture of his loving name, it burns in order to 'refine' (48:10; Mal. 3:2). The fire of God's nature is his passionate, burning love, in that he is determined, at all costs — even at the cost of hell, as we might say — that the gold should be melted out of the alloy 'in the furnace of affliction', in the heat of his love (Isa. 48:10). Then he adds: 'for my own sake, I do it' (v. 11), because I am what I am: passionate love itself.

The statement 'the zeal of the LORD of hosts will do this' (9:7) refers to God's bringing to his throne the messianic king. But 'zeal' (*qinah*) comes from a root which means 'intensely red'. It marks the appearance of the face of the one who intensely, ardently, hotly pursues a course. At 42:13 the RSV translates this term by 'fury'; this meaning occurs also at 59:17, where it is an aspect of God's 'furious' saving love (see 63:15). In every case, therefore, the underlying vision of the term's meaning is 'red-hot'. How very different the Isaian awareness of God as love is from that of many people today whose concept of God as 'love' is weak, insipid, and shallow.

God is the living God; consequently he is the God of action

who extends his 'arm' into human history. Then the casting of fire becomes historical event. This is an issue that puzzles those who examine the NT before studying the OT, which is the original text. They are unable to grasp the historical significance, for example, of the words of John the Baptist about Jesus: 'He will baptize you with the Holy Spirit and with fire' (Matt. 3:11).

One particular basic 'statement of faith' which Israel used throughout the centuries is the Song of Moses (Deuteronomy 32). There at v. 22 we read: 'For a fire is kindled by my anger, and it burns to the depths of Sheol'. We can understand in consequence why the early Church without division of mind included in its creeds the phrase 'He descended into hell'. That clause declares for us that the passionate saving love of God envelopes even what our verse here declares (Isa. 66:15): 'For behold, the LORD will come *in* fire . . . to render the heat of his nostrils, and his rebuke *in* flames of fire' (author's translation). Such then is the eschatological picture of God's furious, re-creative love. It is this which the NT takes over and which it calls 'hell', as it speaks of the love that will not let us go, the love that lays down its life for its friends. But so fierce will be the conflict that there will be many casualties to the heat of the flames. The reality of hell, as a modern writer has put it, is the greatest compliment that the divine can pay to humanity.

Some Little Cameos (17)

We learn from the first cameo what kind of persons Thompson's 'Hound of Heaven' pursues in unrelenting and purifying love. They include 'those who sanctify and purify themselves. . . .' This is what the priest must do before pursuing his holy calling as an intermediary between God and mankind (Exod. 19:20). Yet such was required of all Israel, in their capacity as a kingdom of priests (v. 6; Lev. 11:44). But here Israel's act was a perversion of any preparation to serve the true God.

In the phrase 'to go into the gardens', 'to go' is an addition by the RSV. As we saw at Isa. 65:3, 'the gardens' would be areas amongst the ruins where wild flowers had sprung up (cf. the 'London Pride' that blossomed in the bomb craters of wartime London), and which were then used for the worship of alien and loathsome gods (cf. Ezek. 8:9-10).

Though the text is difficult, the phrase 'following one in the

midst' seems to describe poor, simple, deluded souls blindly but
eagerly repeating the actions of a leader, who would be a kind
of shaman or dervish or medicine man. How common such cults
are today, rising quickly, attracting the disillusioned, and then
fading out. But the point is that these simple folk had freely and
willingly 'sold their souls' to the devilish cult that had attracted
them (cf. Isa. 65:3-4).

The next two cameos are set down side by side with no connecting link — until we meet the last phrase 'says the LORD'. Reality, in the eyes of OT theologians, is one, even as God is one. If
we picture reality as a coin, however, we note that it has two
sides. These sides do not meet, but what is imprinted on the one
side has bearing upon what is on the other side. In the here and
now, 'says the LORD', those apostates in the gardens 'shall come
to an end together'. On the back of the coin, this means that 'by
fire the LORD will execute judgment' — 'in eternity'. The two are
one.

The Great Commission (18-21)

Our editor draws his final chapter to a close by asking us to take
a look at 'the last things'. 'As for me', he lets us hear God say
(the phrase being very emphatic in the Hebrew), 'their works
and their thoughts. . .' That is all we have, so that the sentence
forms an aposiopesis, a sudden breaking off of thought. God's
works and thoughts are totally different from human's, God himself is warning us; DI has already declared this at 55:8. The line
then continues (and all this section is in prose, not verse): 'It has
come' (see RSV mg), in the sense of 'It is sure to come to pass'.
But what is this 'it'? Is it the fulfilment of God's plan, of his
actions and of his thoughts? Whatever 'it' is, the word must refer
to what follows, when God says, 'I am coming to gather all
nations and tongues'. This then is to be an act of the LORD and
not of mankind. It is expressed in a phrase characteristic of the
Aramaic sections of the book of Daniel, and which is common in
intertestamental apocryphal literature.

Thus, 'and they shall come and shall see my glory' will be the
doing of God alone. Isaiah had spoken of 'all the nations' flowing
to Mt. Zion (2:2), the end result of which would be worldwide
shalom. But here we see that mankind will 'flow' thither only
because God is creating the movement. Our passage continues:

All mankind 'shall see my glory', meaning all will obtain the heavenly vision. But even then, the attainment to 'it' will not yet be the end. The end will be an event that can be paralleled with the manner in which Matthew's Gospel finishes.

'And I will set a sign among them' is the same promise with which DI had earlier ended his prophecy (55:12). This is an 'everlasting sign', or better, 'a sign that will last on, because its fulfilment is to be in eternity'. That 'sign' will be the use God will make of his Servant people, the remnant whom he has delivered and saved, and who are now living in full view of the nations of the world. These are the 'survivors', and it is these whom God will 'send to the nations'.

Our author seems to have taken over from Ezekiel the list of nations that follows (Ezek. 27:10, 13; 30:5). And so, as one theologian has put it: 'Those whom God spares will become missionaries to the far world of strange place-names'. There 'the fields are all white', as we might say. They are to go to people 'that have not heard my fame or seen my glory', that is, the story of God's mighty acts and redeeming love. Thus it is only the 'escapees' (*peleytim*) who have been conditioned by God to 'be (or better to 'become', not 'may reach' as RSV) my salvation to the end of the earth' (Isa. 49:6). Only they can pass on God's *tsedaqah*, because only they have known God's *tsedeq* in their own experience of 'resurrection' and renewal. Only they are in the position to declare that King Cyrus was indeed God's 'anointed' instrument to that end (45:1). Only 'they shall declare my glory', or rather 'recount' (*higgid*) it. Only they shall bring 'all your brethren from *amongst* all the nations' (persons such as Mordecai and Queen Esther who dwelt at the court of the Persian monarch?) 'to my holy mountain Jerusalem, says the LORD'.

All these are to come as an 'offering' to God, a *minhah*. This kind of offering was not intended to go up in flames, as was a burnt offering (*'olah*; cf. Gen. 22:3). It was a 'substitute' offering, here evidently for the sins of the Gentiles. The view held by some OT prophets was that at the end all the nations would assemble to be destroyed in one great burnt offering, one great sacrifice (Zeph. 3:8; cf. Joel 3:2; Zech. 14:1-3). Not so the theology of the Isaian tradition. We note that it is not only warrior youths who will come to Jerusalem; the rich too will come in their chariots, pregnant women on their litters (or perhaps 'covered wagons'), the poor upon their mules, the merchants upon dromedaries. The Torah had prescribed that the *minhah* was to be presented 'in a clean vessel to the house of the LORD', in a vessel that had been purified for the service of God's house. What then could 'purified' mean here? We shall see in a moment. At present we note that some of these outlandish foreigners 'I will take for priests and for Levites (or, with the Hebrew, 'for Levitical priests'), says the LORD'. This was an honour not attainable even by ordinary Israelites. The Hebrew word for 'I will take' implies an act that is wholly *ultra vires* ('beyond power'), belonging to the area of 'Behold I make all things new'. For it there is no precedent in the Torah. As Arthur Sumner Herbert has put it: 'This is in very truth [a sign of] a new heaven and a new earth'! (*Isaiah 40-66*, 197).

22-23 What will 'remain' therefore is that for which God, in the beginning, began to create (Gen. 1:1 RSV mg), namely a new people. Throughout time he brought into being — he created or, as we have now learned to translate the word, he re-created (*bara*) — his people, from a 'no-people' to his own possession (Isa. 43:15). But now they had gone through a new metamorphosis; they were children, 'brought forth in one moment' (Isa. 66:8). Yet it was not an unexpected act of God. He had declared he would do so in the beginning, when he began to make the heavens and the earth (51:16). Consequently, TI is in the position to tell us that God's love for his people and the forgiveness inherent in his nature actually belong in eternity. Because this is so, God's beloved and forgiven people too will necessarily 'remain' to all eternity. For, 'God's sustaining creativity' is evidently what Paul Tillich declared to be another name for grace. The *peleytim*, the 'survivors', the 'resurrected from the grave of Babylon' (Ezekiel 37), therefore could now possess the glad assurance that they had indeed inherited eternal life. They were persuaded of this because God's re-creative love had now been acted out in history — now, in their lifetime and experience — so that their eternal destiny was no mere speculative philosophical hope.

The end that this chapter deals with then is not merely something to happen in the distant future. It has happened now, because it has been an act of the eternal God. It is an event that, since it has occurred in history, speaks of the greatness and eternity of God's loving purpose for human life. If we today hope to understand Isaian theology, we must rid ourselves from the influence of speculative 'Greek' thought and of the millenarian sects that have flourished down the centuries. One such end and resurrection had now occurred in history, that foreseen by Amos in 760 B.C. (Amos 8:2). Consequently, the end and then the resurrection that took place in A.D. 33 — of God's people Israel once again, but now in the person of one representative Israelite — is to be understood as the ultimate revelation of the nature and purpose of the living God.

The new heavens and the new earth are now described finally in terms of God's own sabbath, God's eternal rest (Gen. 2:3). In that sabbath 'all flesh shall come to worship before me, says the LORD', a reality which he had promised already through the lips of DI (Isa. 45:23).

24   Yet, since biblical theologians point to the fact that there are in the world three categories of persons, how then can 'all flesh come to worship before me'? These categories are God's redeemed people; God's 'poor', the masses of humanity of all races, colours, tongues, and religions; and God's enemies, the vicious, the negative, the destructive, the ruthless egoists — in fact, those who have 'sinned against the Holy Spirit' (as Matt. 12:32 interprets 11:21-22). It is to this last group, then, that this last verse of the whole book of Isaiah is directed.

That 'hell' includes the concept of separation from God through the disintegration of the human personality is revealed to us in the autobiographical report of the young Isaiah in Isaiah 6. There he exclaims in horror, 'Woe is me! For I am *disintegrated* (as the Hebrew means)', finally 'lost' and annihilated (6:5). That terrible experience, like the reason behind the cry of desolation at Ps. 22:1, God answered; but he answered by grace alone, as we see when we read on. Isaiah could do nothing for himself; he had reached the 'end'. But God sent, as an extension of himself, a burning emissary (the meaning of *seraph*), 'having in his hand a burning coal which he had taken with tongs' (because it was too hot, with the heat of God himself, even for a 'burning angel' to hold in his hand, though he himself was a flame of fire; cf. Ps. 104:4) 'from the altar' — that is, from the very heart of God (Isa. 6:6). It was that terrible act of God which actually recreated Isaiah from dissolution, from being returned to *tohu*, to 'chaos', to negation (cf. Jer. 4:25). It was of course forgiveness that created the renewal: 'Your guilt is taken away, and your sin forgiven' (Isa. 6:7). It is not time or space that separates people from God; it is sin. But God's 'mission' does not end here. At once he sends Isaiah in mission to his people, Israel, even as he sends Israel to the world at 66:19. That which the young Isaiah had experienced existentially was, of course, an act of God. And so the reality of newness which he met with belonged with the eternal God in eternity. In other words, it 'remained' (v. 22).

TI can thus confidently draw to a conclusion his 'completion' of the whole Isaian theology into which he had been born. He does so by making plain the one reality that God has in store for all people. Mankind may suppose — even redeemed Israel may suppose — that death is the 'end' of the wicked. Just to the southwest of the city and over Jerusalem's wall there burned night and day in the valley of Hinnom the rubbish dump of the city. But there was more to the smell from it than that of rubbish, for along with that went the terrible smell of roasting flesh. Jerusalem's citizens could go outside for a walk at any time, 'go forth and look on the dead bodies' there of unwanted babies, convicts, suicides, and all such as were beyond the pale, outside the covenant. The historical *Ge-hinnom*, which becomes 'Gehenna' in NT Greek, was thus of eschatological significance because it revealed the severity of the judgment of God here and now and always. In fact, it was a kind of acted parable of the terrible reality of the eternal judgment of God.

But TI knew that obliteration in its fires cannot be the 'end' of the wicked, for it had not been the final end of the sinful young man Isaiah; and God does not change over the generations. The end can only be God himself, for he is the first and the last (44:6). In her life of G. K. Chesterton, Maisie Ward quotes from one of his novels: 'What you call evil I call good. I stopped, startled; as I passed the fire, I did not know whether it was hell or the furious love of God'.

As Isaiah had said at 9:7, the zeal of the LORD, his 'burning' perfectionism, would inevitably bring about the consummation of the divine plan, that every knee should bow to him (45:23). The love of the God of Isaian theology is inexorable, for it is predetermined (51:16). It is known throughout the OT by the Hebrew word *hesed*, which the RSV translates as 'steadfast love'; for it is the love that will not let us go.

POSTSCRIPT

Many theological issues arise from the above chapters to affect both Jews and Christians, and by implication, Muslims as well. We draw attention to some of these.

(1) We note that the word 'Jew' never occurs in the whole book of Isaiah, not even in the historical insets. This name associated with the People of God first appears in the book of Jeremiah, but only after the deportation to Babylon. The deported Israelites were only one group out of many displaced persons from amongst whom they had necessarily to distinguish themselves before the officials of the Babylonian government. They could scarcely call themselves 'the People of Yahweh', 'the People of the Covenant', or even merely 'Israel' while they dwelt in Babylon, in that all three of these titles were theological in content. So they chose for themselves the name 'Judah-ites', which in English becomes 'Jews'. The name 'Jew' is thus an ethnic title, and is not theological as is 'Israel'. TI was aware that 'our father Abraham' was not a Jew but a Gentile. The Israelites of the Exodus had been a 'mixed multitude' (Exod. 12:19, 38), and in the days of Joshua great numbers of Canaanites had joined Israel, that is, had become members of the People of God.

Of course, TI too would have had to call himself a Jew while still in Babylon, but only to the authorities whom he had to obey. We note that he does not call himself or his fellow returnees by that name in these chapters, all of which were uttered once he was back 'home' in Zion. TI knows that he and they were all members of a theocratic society, rooted in God's choice of Abraham, with God as Father and with Zion as Mother. Moreover, he shows that all peoples, races, nations, and tongues are invited to join with him in God's 'covenant fellowship'; he did not expect them to become 'Jews'.

The book of Ezra, which tells of the Return to Zion, is basically

120

a historical document. In it, Ezra reverts to the use of the term 'Jew'. TI, on the other hand, gives no historical references whatsoever. He is not speaking or writing as a historian about a people known to history as Jews; his concern is with the work of God over the space of two hundred years in and through God's covenant people for the sake of the whole world of mankind.

Thus the book of Isaiah is not a 'Jewish book', as has only too often been declared. It is a book of revelation meant for all who come after, whether Jew or Christian. It thus provides the Jew, the Christian, and the Muslim with a common basis for faith, and in this way forms a meeting place for all three faiths.

(2) The amazing wholeness of the theology of 'Isaiah' alerts us to the folly of seeking to formulate a Christology or indeed a theology of the New Testament of any kind without reference to the Old Testament. Such an attempt must by its very nature be false, for it ignores — and thus acts in rebellion (*pesha'*, Isaiah's word) against — the Covenant which binds all the acts of God from Abraham to Paul into a purposeful, developing, and creative whole. TI in particular, as the apex or crown of the book's sixty-six chapters, provides us with an insight into the nature of God that requires only the person of Christ to incarnate it and so to make it complete, and to perform it on the cross and so to render it effectual for all time and for eternity.

It is clear from the Gospels that Jesus set little store by the office of Messiah, which some modern theologians imagine to be his calling from God. Anyone can be a 'messiah': priest, prophet, or even pagan king. What Jesus says of himself is that he is 'I AM', and that even before Abraham was he is 'I AM'. Thus if Jesus is hailed merely as 'the Messiah of the Jews', then the content of that book over which the Ethiopian eunuch (Acts 8:26-28) was puzzling has been completely misunderstood.

'Isaiah' provides us with a picture, a pattern of revelation, hewn out of the facts of history. It is a picture of God's saving love for mankind within the Covenant that he himself has given to the world in and through his historical, factual, empirical people Israel. This means that, if 'Isaiah' has indeed produced a true theology, then our biblical faith is based, not on speculation, but on fact.

(3) In *The Origin and Goal of History*, Karl Jaspers declares that in the period about 550-500 B.C. we find the rise of what he

121

names 'axial man'. According to Jaspers, the 'axial religions' that developed into Hinduism, Buddhism, Confucianism, Zoroastrianism, and others in the Near East, even including Greece, all began with a great urge in mankind to search for God and to find salvation for the human soul. Only Israel, we can see, of all the peoples of the known world, thought otherwise. Israel's spokesmen in that period were Deutero- and Trito-Isaiah, along with the priestly group of scholars who were then completing the book of Leviticus.

We can see how the 'Isaian' prophets ignored this world movement. They declared, and only they, that mankind had no need to search for God, because God had already found mankind, in that he had already broken through the barrier that exists between the divine and the human by forgiving mankind for the sin which separates them from God. Mankind in consequence was now able to *shub* ('come back', 'repent'), thereby rendering irrelevant any kind of search for God.

Sinful mankind had only to accept God's gracious offer of life and to enter the Covenant that God had first initiated with his 'peculiar' people — peculiar because they alone were not 'axial man'. Those already within the Covenant were then to show to 'axial man' that God had found them too.

That, then, was TI's basic insight. Parallel with it, moreover, was the priestly understanding of the Covenant. The book of Leviticus shows all people, both those born within the Covenant and those who enter from without, how they may *stay* within it and so continue to possess the fellowship of God.

The law of the Covenant, TI shows, is a demanding one. It demands trust and obedience; for it is only in obedience that a person finds life and joy. That is why the offer of the law is accompanied by a threat to all who contract out of it. If a person does so, then the covenant partner turns into an opponent. It is God's faithfulness to the Covenant that obliges him to be a jealous God. God is therefore bound to be against those who refuse to accept his will for equal justice for all his creatures, equal distribution of the land, equal access to the sources of food, drink, and clothing. The foreigner, 'coming in' from outside, 'who has joined himself to the LORD', must necessarily learn all this. Consequently it is for those already 'in' to teach the stranger about the will of God. What is required of the 'resurrected', the 'new' Israel, is not so much to show 'faith' as to live in 'faithfulness'.

The result of this demand is that the book of Isaiah ends with the terrible threat that, while all people are indeed under the judgment of God, Israel is to recognize that the reality is something that Amos had discovered two centuries before. Speakiŋ g for God himself, Amos had declared to the 'chosen', the covenant people, 'You only have I known of all the families of the earth; therefore I will punish you. . .' (Amos 3:2). In later centuries the NT expresses the same truth from the mouth of him who was to be the Church's Rock: 'For the time has come for judgment to begin with the household of God' (1 Pet. 4:17). This basic element in the gospel is one that many believers today are unwilling to face.

(4) Finally, in TI's work we have much emphasis laid upon *the land*. The land marks the 'living space' which is God's gift to his covenant people. That is why TI expresses God's redemptive purpose by making use of what today we would call 'sacramental' language. Israel's land is the great 'sacrament' of the Covenant. In fact, it has always been so ever since the days of Joshua, even since the divine promise made to Abraham. But, as in the case of Hosea before him (Hos. 2:18-20), our prophet draws no line between God's dealings with Israel's 'person' as his bride and loved one and his dealing with nature, the land, the physical world. We should keep in mind here that the word for 'land' can equally well mean 'earth' or even 'created matter', as we see at Gen. 1:10. TI is no Platonic philosopher, separating soul from body, mankind from their environment, even as did the mystery religions also in the early Christian centuries. Thus TI would have been able to appreciate fully the assertion in the NT that 'the Word became flesh'. Then again, since the human person is in fact one with his or her environment, as a social being that person derives presuppositions from the society which gave him birth. And since a person's body is composed of 'the bread and the wine' which grows out of the land (as Hosea 2), the new heaven and new earth, or 'land', must necessarily contribute to the new person's wholeness. This is the wholeness not only of the New Jerusalem, but also of the One who epitomises the resurrected Israel in the world to come (Isa. 65:17; John 20:24-29).

SELECTED BIBLIOGRAPHY

Commentaries

Achtemeier, E. *The Community and Message of Isaiah 56 – 66: A Theological Commentary* (Minneapolis: Augsburg, 1982).

Hamlin, E. J. *Comfort My People: A Guide to Isaiah 40 – 66* (Atlanta: John Knox, 1979).

Herbert, A. S. *The Book of the Prophet Isaiah, Chapters 40 – 66.* Cambridge Bible Commentary (Cambridge: University Press, 1975).

Holladay, W. L. *Isaiah: Scroll of a Prophetic Heritage* (Grand Rapids: Wm. B. Eerdmans, 1978).

Jones, D. R. *Isaiah 56 – 66 and Joel.* Torch Bible Commentary (London: SCM, 1964).

Knight, G. A. F. *Prophets of Israel: Isaiah.* Bible Guides (New York: Abingdon, 1961).

Muilenberg, J. 'The Book of Isaiah, Chapters 56 – 66: Introduction and Exegesis', *Interpreter's Dictionary of the Bible* 5:652-773.

Pauritsch, K. *Die neue Gemeinde: Gott sammelt Ausgestossene und Arme (Jesaja 56 – 66).* Analecta Biblica 47 (Rome: Biblical Institute Press, 1971).

Skinner, J. *The Book of the Prophet Isaiah,* Vol. 2: *Isaiah 40 – 66.* Cambridge Bible (1898; reprint ed. Cambridge: University Press, 1958).

Smith, G. A. *The Book of Isaiah,* Vol. 2: XL – LXVI. Expositor's Bible (1890; reprint ed. Grand Rapids: Wm. B. Eerdmans, 1956) 3:748-846.

Westermann, C. *Isaiah 40 – 66: A Commentary.* Old Testament Library (Philadelphia: Westminster and London: SCM, 1969).

Whitehouse, O. C. *Isaiah,* Vol. 2: *XL – LXVI.* Century Bible (1908; reprint ed. Edinburgh: T. C. and E. C. Jack, 1931).

Whybray, R. N. *Isaiah 40 – 66.* New Century Bible Commentary (Grand Rapids: Wm. B. Eerdmans, 1981).

Wildberger, H. *Jesaja.* Biblischer Kommentar: Altes Testament (Neukirchen-Vluyn: Neukirchener Verlag, 1970–).

Other Works

Ackroyd, P. R. *Exile and Restoration: A Study of Hebrew Thought of the Sixth Century B.C.* Old Testament Library (Philadelphia: Westminster and London: SCM, 1968).
Barth, K. *Church Dogmatics*, 4 vols. in 13 (Edinburgh: T. & T. Clark, 1955-1969).
Berkhof, H. *Christian Faith: An Introduction to the Study of the Faith*, trans. S. Woudstra (Grand Rapids: Wm. B. Eerdmans, 1979).
Bonhoeffer, D. *Christ the Center*, trans. J. Bowden (New York: Harper & Row, 1966).
Clark, K. *Civilisation* (London: British Broadcasting Corporation and New York: Harper & Row, 1969).
Cohn, N. *Europe's Inner Demons: An Enquiry Inspired by the Great Witch-Hunt* (New York: Basic Books, 1975).
Driver, G. R. 'Difficult Words in the Hebrew Prophets', in *Studies in Old Testament Prophecy*, ed. H. H. Rowley (Edinburgh: T. & T. Clark, 1950), 52-72.
Foster, R. S. *The Restoration of Israel: A Study in Exile and Return* (London: Darton, Longman & Todd, 1970).
Frost, S. B. *Old Testament Apocalyptic* (London: Epworth, 1952).
Hanson, P. D. *The Dawn of Apocalyptic* (Philadelphia: Fortress, 1975).
Jaspers, K. *The Origin and Goal of History*, trans. M. Bullock (London: Routledge & Kegan Paul, 1953).
Knight, G. A. F. 'The Protestant World and Mariology', *Scottish Journal of Theology* 19 (1966): 55-73.
————. *Theology as Narration: A Commentary on the Book of Exodus* (Edinburgh: Handsel and Grand Rapids: Wm. B. Eerdmans, 1976).
Koch, K. *The Prophets*, Vol. 2: *The Babylonian and Persian Periods* (Philadelphia: Fortress, 1984).
Lind, M. C. *Yahweh Is a Warrior* (Scottdale: Herald, 1980).
Neusner, J. *First Century Judaism in Crisis* (Nashville: Abingdon, 1975).
Ozment, S. *The Age of Reform 1250–1550* (New Haven: Yale University Press, 1980).
Pritchard, J. B., ed. *Ancient Near Eastern Texts Relating to the Old Testament*, 3rd ed. (Princeton: Princeton University Press, 1969).
Raitt, T. M. *A Theology of Exile* (Philadelphia: Fortress, 1977).
Sanders, E. P., ed. *Jewish and Christian Self-Definition*, Vol. 2: *Aspects of Judaism in the Greco-Roman Period* (Philadelphia: Fortress, 1981).

Simon, U. E. *A Theology of Auschwitz: The Christian Faith and the Problem of Evil* (Atlanta: John Knox, 1979).

Smart, J. D. *History and Theology in Second Isaiah* (Philadelphia: Westminster, 1965).

Stone, M. E. 'Coherence and Inconsistency in the Apocalypses: The Case of "the End" ', *Journal of Biblical Literature* 102 (1983): 229-43.

Tillich, P. *Systematic Theology*, 3 vols. in 1 (Chicago: University of Chicago Press, 1967).

Torrance, D. W., ed. *The Witness of the Jews to God* (Edinburgh: Handsel, 1982).

von Rad, G. *Old Testament Theology*, 2 vols., trans. D. M. G. Stalker (Edinburgh: Oliver & Boyd and New York: Harper & Row, 1962-1965).

Ward, M. *Gilbert Keith Chesterton* (London: Sheed & Ward, 1944).

Zimmerli, W. *Zur Sprache Tritojesajes*. Schweizerische Theologische Umschau 20 (1950): 110-22; reprinted in *Gottes Offenbarung*. Gesammelte Aufsätze zum Alten Testament. Theologische Bücherei 19 (1963): 217-33.